MULTIRACIALS AND CIVIL RIGHTS

Multiracials and Civil Rights

Mixed-Race Stories of Discrimination

Tanya Katerí Hernández

NEW YORK UNIVERSITY PRESS

New York

NEW YORK UNIVERSITY PRESS
New York
www.nyupress.org

First published in paperback in 2021

Portions of chapters 1 and 2 were published as "Multiracial in the Workplace: A New Kind of Discrimination?" in *Gender, Race, and Ethnicity in the Workplace: Emerging Issues and Enduring Challenges*, ed. Margaret Foegen Karsten. ABC-CLIO, 2016: 3–25; copyright 2016. Reprinted by permission.

A portion of chapter 6 was published as "Racially-Mixed Personal Identity Equality," in *Law, Culture and the Humanities*, vol 15 (2017):1–11; copyright 2017. Reprinted by permission.

References to Internet websites (URLs) were accurate at the time of writing. Neither the author nor New York University Press is responsible for URLs that may have expired or changed since the manuscript was prepared.

Library of Congress Cataloging-in-Publication Data
Names: Hernández, Tanya Katerí, author.
Title: Multiracials and civil rights : mixed-race stories of discrimination /
Tanya Katerí Hernández.
Description: New York : New York University Press, [2018] |
Includes bibliographical references and index.
Identifiers: LCCN 2017044874 | ISBN 978-1-4798-3032-9 (cl : alk. paper)
| ISBN 978-1-4798-3032-1 (cl : alk. paper) ISBN 978-1-4798-0606-5 (pb : alk. paper)
Subjects: LCSH: Race discrimination—Law and legislation—United States. | Colorism—United States. | Racially mixed people—Civil rights—United States. | United States—Race relations.
Classification: LCC KF4755 .H47 2018 | DDC 342.7308/73—dc23
LC record available at https://lccn.loc.gov/2017044874

New York University Press books are printed on acid-free paper, and their binding materials are chosen for strength and durability. We strive to use environmentally responsible suppliers and materials to the greatest extent possible in publishing our books.

Manufactured in the United States of America

10 9 8 7 6 5 4 3 2 1

Also available as an ebook

For my Mother,

my beloved model for being a no-nonsense race woman,

and for Alesandro and Leila,

my lifelong inspirations for trying to illuminate the

ongoing operation of racism and the way forward.

CONTENTS

An Afro-Latina's Experience of Racial Mixture

Pure breeds (at least the black ones) are out and hybridity is in. . . . Major news magazines announce our arrival as if we were proof of extraterrestrial life. They claim we're going to bring about the end of race as we know it. . . . being a fetishized object, an exotic bird soaring above the racial landscape.
—Danzy Senna, "Mulatto Millennium"[1]

I am the mixed-race daughter of a mixed-race mother almost given away because of her blackness. Thus, regardless of how much my professional life as a lawyer guides my interest in the topic of civil rights law, I know that my family history of race is the soil from which I have grown into a scholar-activist. More importantly for this book, my family story of race is also my barometer for assessing how much group narratives about racial mixture affect opportunity.

In the 1940s, my maternal grandmother Lucrecia was a "country girl," or what her fellow Puerto Ricans called a "*jíbara*," from a mountain village in Puerto Rico.[2] Her African ancestry appeared slightly in her *trigueña* (light wheat color) skin tone but was not very apparent in her facial features or hair texture. Her older sisters were similarly light-skinned and favored their fair-complected mother more than their darker-skinned father. For this reason Lucrecia and her sisters considered themselves a race apart from those who appeared more unambiguously Afro-descended. Any tinge of color in the family was attributed to the long-ago legacy of Taíno Indians on the island. It was immaterial to the family that Taíno Indians were documented to have been exterminated by Spanish conquerors by the mid-sixteenth century.[3]

When my grandmother Lucrecia fell in love with and united herself with carpenter and guitarist Juan, her family was not pleased. While he was a mixed-race grandchild of a former slave, and son of an Afro–Puerto Rican mother and white Spaniard, his darker appearance was what Lucrecia's family labeled as "black" and thus unacceptable. Puerto Rican identity may claim to celebrate racial mixture, but some of us are thought to "look" more mixed than others. Dark-skin deviations from the idealization of light skin with European features and straight hair are ejected from the Puerto Rican portrait of racial mixture. Lucrecia's family was no exception to this Puerto Rican (and Latin American) anti-black conception of racial mixture.[4]

Infidelity eventually caused further strain on their union, and Lucrecia's older sisters encouraged her to leave Juan and migrate to New York. Hoping to teach Juan a lesson and have him mend his ways, Lucrecia secretly boarded a ship from Puerto Rico to New York in the early 1940s with her two-year-old daughter. She was unknowingly three months pregnant with a second child and entertained the romantic notion that Juan would chase her to New York and commit himself to being faithful. Feeling abandoned and hurt himself, Juan never did follow her to New York City. Lucrecia did not inform him of the birth of his second child until the child was approximately eight years old.

Lucrecia's second child, Nina (my mother), was born in the 1940s, and much to the dismay of Lucrecia's family, they considered the child dark. Too dark. Too dark to count as racially mixed and certainly too dark to be presented as a "white" Puerto Rican. Baby Nina did not pass the "look behind the ears" Caribbean test of seeking out future darkness of infants.[5] Even more problematic, Nina's skin tone (approximating that of 1940s African American singer and actress Lena Horne—the Beyoncé of her time) would complicate the family's image as disassociated from blackness. The campaign to send baby Nina away began in earnest. Lucrecia's family lobbied to have baby Nina placed for adoption with an African American family. Any African American family would do as long as baby Nina was removed from the household. Only as an adult researcher would I later learn from a colleague how much the family impulse paralleled the dynamic in Puerto Rico of returning foster children like damaged goods when they become "too dark."[6]

At the same time, the family's animus towards the Afro–Puerto Rican father that baby Nina favored did not extend to her older sister, Mónica. Mónica was lighter in complexion with long, straight hair. Mónica's African ancestry did not announce itself so loudly in her appearance, and she was immediately accepted by the family. The physical comparison between the two sisters was a constant obsession of the family, with Nina being called "*monito*" (little monkey) and "*negrita bembe*" (little black African-like girl), while Mónica was simply called "*la nena*" (the little girl).

Lucrecia ultimately refused to succumb to the family pressure to have baby Nina given away, but she never let Nina forget it. It is uncertain whether Lucrecia refused to give Nina away because she still entertained the hope that her partner would swoop in from Puerto Rico for a reunification or whether her refusal was rooted in a semblance of maternal affection. What is irrefutable is that Lucrecia viewed Nina's darker skin tone and African tresses as problematic. Her kinky curls—*pelo malo* (bad hair)—was a source of consternation that compelled Lucrecia to continually shave baby Nina's hair in the hope that it would grow out straighter. Any infraction of Lucrecia's rules of discipline was greeted with both a beating and an expression of regret for not having given her away to an African American family at birth, along with the threat to place Nina in a foster home.

This was a marked contrast to the indulgence accorded her older sister, Mónica, who had slightly lighter skin and, more importantly, straighter *pelo lindo* (pretty hair), preferred as "good hair." Even milk in the home was rationed across a color line. Lucrecia's mother, my great-grandmother, would allocate the milk in the home to Mónica and give Nina water instead. Birthday party celebrations were reserved for Mónica alone. Unlike for Mónica, light-colored nail polish was forbidden for Nina lest her hands look even darker. The racialized distinctions between the two girls continued their entire lives.

The pain of family rejection based on her apparent African ancestry was so profound for my mother that she shared her stories with me very early on. My own childhood experiences with differential treatment based on how "mixed" or "black" I looked on any given day or in any given context only reinforced my understanding of the relevance of anti-black sentiment within celebrations of idealized notions of mixture. My appearance reflects the mixture of my mother Nina's Afro–Puerto Rican physical traits and my father's white-skinned background. While slightly lighter in skin shade than my mother, the brownness of my skin would never cause anyone to view me as white. Many have told me that I am a doppelganger for their various relatives in India. However, the comparison to relatives in India often disappears depending on what my hair decides to do that day. On a low humidity day with enough hair care products to make my hair lie down and be wrestled into a curl-hiding bun, I look more Indian. If I let it out and allow the curls to reign supreme, my African ancestry is more apparent to others.

How much of my perspective on the meaning of race might have diverged had my hair been different, I wonder? My grandmother Lucrecia was never happier than when my hair was greased down into two long braids down my back and I looked like what she envisioned as an indigenous Taína. But her absolute preference was for me to have my hair blow-dried straight regardless of how short in duration the look would last (one day in humid weather, or maybe a week with the aid of large rollers, dry air, and a nightly *dubi* scalp wrapping of the hair for maximum stretch). However, the Hair Wars began in earnest when I cut off my hair in an act of adolescent rebellion. My grandmother was mystified as to why I would choose to have my curls spring out on display in what resembled my mother's afro. In my grandmother's eyes, my mother was unfortunately afflicted with overtly "bad hair," but why in the world would I choose to emulate that style when I had the "benefit" of being better situated to beat my hair into submission with a "more attractive" simulation of whiteness? Every visit to her apartment on the

Lower East Side of Manhattan was greeted with some version of "*ay ese pelo*" (oh that hair) or "*porque no haces algo con ese pelo*?" (why don't you do something with that hair?).

Wearing my hair in a short, curly mop also worked to seemingly eject me from my presumed membership in the Latino imaginary. Encountering Latino merchants and other Latino service providers, I was now constantly greeted with a surprised "oh you speak Spanish" and "where did you learn to speak Spanish?" My hair now barred the door to my automatic entrée to Latino kinship.[7] I now had to earn my way back into Latinaness by constantly speaking Spanish loudly and referencing my Latina culture. As in Latin America, the imagined Latino community had and has a decided vision of mixture that does not encompass tightly coiled hair with brown skin. The anti-black slurs I heard used in the Latino community with respect to African Americans only reinforced my early impressions that blackness was problematic despite our assertions of Latino pride in being a mixture of races. It became evident to me that cultural *mestizaje* pride (race mixture pride) aside, not all parts of the mixture were equally welcomed or celebrated.[8]

When I became older and took on the role of translating government forms into Spanish for my grandmother, our disputes about race escalated into the Census Conflict. In the 1980s she was fine with responding "yes" to the question of whether her ethnicity was of Hispanic origin. After I translated the census question, she told me to check the Hispanic-origin ethnicity box "Yes." But when it came to the separate question regarding racial ancestry, she became agitated and wanted us to just skip the question. Being an argumentative teenager with control over the English-language form, I insisted that she engage with the category options of white, black, Native American, Asian, or other. Screaming matches ensued as she demanded that I insert "Boricua" (Puerto Rican) as a race into the Some Other Race slot, and I insisted that Puerto Rican is not a race unto itself. If we were so proud of being racially mixed Puerto Ricans, why not list all parts of the mixture on the Some Other Race line? That was unacceptable to her.

By the time the census forms were modified in 2000 to permit multiple-box-checking responses to the racial category question, she was living in a nursing home, unable to communicate in any language about government forms. Yet everything about her lifelong aversion to attributing her light brown skin to African ancestry and her preference for evading discussions about the specifics of her ancestry in lieu of emphasizing the unenumerated racial mixture of Puerto Rican identity tells me that she would have been uninterested in the ability to check multiple racial boxes, let alone the black box.

Even outside of the family nucleus I found that there was a politics to racial mixture that living in the multiethnic New York City of the late 1960s and 1970s did not abate. I was blessed to have attended the dynamic Bank Street Head Start program located in the Midtown West neighborhood of Manhattan (then known as Hell's Kitchen and the backdrop for the play and film *West Side Story*). The preschool was incredibly diverse and a delight to attend. (If any of those Bank Street Head Start teachers are now reading this—thank you for all you did to animate my life of learning!) However, when we all "graduated" preschool and enrolled in elementary school together, I was separated from my diverse group of friends. For the first two weeks of first grade I found myself in a chaotic classroom where we were often left unattended and where very little learning took place. Welcome to the special education class of the 1960s.

The class was filled with brown-skinned Latinos and African Americans I had never met before. I was separated from my best friend, Lizzie, with the sweet white Irish face. I was separated from my Puerto Rican buddy, Ruben of the pale white skin and dark brown eyes. Nor were any of the other paler-skinned Puerto Ricans from Head Start in the special ed class with me.

When my mother discovered that something was not quite right about my elementary school learning situation, she intervened, and the school official claimed I was placed there because of my Spanish-language education needs—an explanation that was most peculiar given the English-dominant African Americans in the class and the absence of any bilingual education offered while I was there. Back then there was not a public conversation about the school-to-prison pipeline, but there was certainly a penitentiary approach to warehousing difference. Only when my mother insisted that English was my primary language and the language of my instruction in preschool was I able to enter a mainstream classroom where actual teaching took place.

Even after my escape from the special education of the 1960s (which was neither special nor an education), my New York City public school education continued to operate within a pigmentocracy wherein the racial mixture of Latinos was acknowledged but closer approximations of whiteness were rewarded with presumptions of competence and intellect. This became especially clear to me when strangers did not know my Spanish surname or ethnic origin and presumed that my black-white mixture was solely due to an African American ancestry. My pen pal from rural Pennsylvania provided me with that invaluable insight.

I was so excited when the Scholastic book company offered to pair fellow book readers as pen pals in elementary school. My pen pal and I exchanged letters for months and promised to visit one another to learn more about the urban/rural differences that interested us. She repeatedly asked for a photograph, but I wanted to make a good impression and send her the school pictures scheduled to be taken later in the year. She sent me her picture with a sweet smile in a white face and long, straight, brown hair. Our pen pal friendship deepened until the moment she received my photograph. While she previously was unperturbed about writing to a Hernández, she refused to have anything further to do with a brown-skinned Hernández regardless of where my degree of pigment fell on the mixed-race spectrum.

The sharp termination of that pen pal friendship left an indelible mark of racial rejection. Over time I was unable to compartmentalize it as a rejection limited to sheltered rural dwellers. Becoming the recipient in the 1970s of an A Better Chance scholarship to attend an elite private prep school taught me that racial ignorance resided in the urbane environs of the Upper East Side of Manhattan as well. There were countless moments when the predominantly white student population of the high school ("upper school," in private school jargon) made me feel keenly my difference as a nonwhite scholarship student. I bonded tightly with the few other African American students who felt similarly isolated. The school administration was uniformly supportive until the moment for the submission of college applications arrived.

The school college advisor met with each of us to counsel us as to the best array of college application options. I was strongly advised to apply to a New York state school, and my African American friends were steered towards historically black colleges. This was not the same advice that our white counterparts at the school received; each of them was instead encouraged to reach for at least one star college. Ivy League schools were not on the table for discussion with me and the other nonwhite students despite the school's status as a "feeder" to the Ivy League. Irrespective of our fortitude in surviving the transition to the rarified "preppy" private high school environment, we were not viewed as "good fits" for the Ivy League circle. The "degree" of our blackness or ethnicity was immaterial. We were all lumped together as noncontenders. When an Ivy League university solicited my application and the admissions officer who interviewed me encouraged me to apply, the racial hierarchy of my prep-school college-advising program came into sharp relief.

Being admitted to and attending an elite university in the 1980s was a transformative experience for me, yet it was no racial utopia. During the fall semester of my freshman year, a number of racial incidents occurred that culminated in beer bottles being thrown at black women from the windows of the fraternity houses on campus. Racial epithets accompanied the violence. Regardless of our shade or mixture, many of us never again felt safe walking past frat row.

I share this compressed mini-biography of race for the sole purpose of explaining why this book came about. Many other incidents could have been included. But my aim here is not to compose a memoir. After a lifetime of seeing how my mixed-race and multiethnic status did not shield me from the racism of our society (nor many others I traveled to), it came as a surprise to me to read the work of legal scholars proclaiming that mixed-race racial discrimination was distinct in nature from the racial discrimination that non-multiracial-identified persons experience. While certainly every individual perceives racial discrimination as his or her own personal experience, it was a jolt to encounter the premise that the presumed uniqueness of the discrimination against multiracial-identified persons required a new approach to civil rights law. Because this presumption is such a disconnect from my own mixed-race experience with race, I began a journey of tracking down the multiracial accounts of racism for myself. This book thus examines the narratives of mixed-race-identified persons bringing claims of racial discrimination in court. The story of white privilege that unfolds is unfortunately not unique. However, the tale of why multiracial discrimination is thought to challenge traditional understandings of civil rights law has much to teach us about how to move towards a more egalitarian society. It is my hope that the insights I found in examining the multiracial discrimination cases will be illuminating for you as well, whatever your own story of race may be.

1

Racial Mixture as a Presumed Complication in Antidiscrimination Law

Impurity and hybridity, in and of themselves, are no guaranteed challenge to the racial orders of white supremacy and antiblackness.
—Jared Sexton, *Amalgamation Schemes*[1]

In 2016, Cleon Brown thought it would be fun to take the Ancestry.com test. Cleon appeared to the world as white, and all forty-seven years of his life had been lived as white man. But he was curious to seek out confirmation of the Native American ancestry rumored to be in his family as well. He was thus surprised when the test results indicated that there was zero Native American ancestry, and instead 18 percent Saharan African ancestry. Cleon shared the news with his fellow police officers, and the racist commentary began in earnest. He was called "Kunta" after the fictional slave in the *Roots* book and television series. More racial commentary and harassment followed. He was excluded from police sergeant training, mandatory Taser instructor recertification training, along with police department business meetings. Eventually Cleon was asked to resign as sergeant and return to the lower status of patrol officer. Eighteen years of collegial work together as police officers was immaterial in the face of the knowledge of Cleon's distant African ancestry. Cleon's white appearance and life as a white man was irrelevant to his racial harassers. All that mattered was his known affiliation, however slight, with the racial category of blackness and his newfound status as a nonwhite, racially mixed person.

Ancestry.com thus introduced Cleon to the world of multiracial discrimination. His lawsuit against the police department followed in 2017, and was still pending at the time of this writing.[2] According to the Federal Bureau of Investigation, Cleon is not the only multiracial victim of racial hatred. In 2015 alone, 3.8 percent of victims of hate crimes were multiracial.[3] This book seeks to illuminate what it means for civil rights law when and how mixed-race persons experience racial discrimination.

The growth of a mixed-race population in the United States that identifies itself as "multiracial" has commanded public attention. With the 2000 Census, the U.S. Census Bureau began permitting respondents to simultaneously select multiple racial categories to designate their multiracial backgrounds. With the release of data for both the 2000 and 2010 census years, much media attention has followed the fact that first 2.4 percent, then 2.9 percent of the population selected two or more races.[4] The Census Bureau projects that the self-identified multiracial population will triple by 2060.[5] Yet mixed-race peoples are not new. Demographer Ann Morning points out that their presence in North America was noted in colonial records as early as the 1630s.[6]

Nevertheless, scholars have documented how the mainstream press has universally celebrated the growth of a multiracial-identified population as a new phenomenon that portends "the end of race as we know it."[7] Indeed, advertisers have seized upon the interest in what sociologist Kimberly McClain DaCosta describes as "racially ambiguous" and presumably mixed-race-appearing persons for marketing numerous products.[8] Ethnic studies scholar Caroline Streeter notes that the ubiquity of media images featuring mixed-race people as visions of racial harmony is a device that "emphasizes the pleasurable aspects of ethnic diversity without engaging the challenge of cultural differences and the existence of racial hierarchies and racial inequality. Multicultural images that use multiracial people envision a future free of such power struggles."[9]

The public fascination with multiracial identity has promoted the belief that racial mixture will, in and of itself, destroy racism. For instance, leaders of the lobby for recognition of a "multiracial" census category frequently posit that multiracials are a "unifying force,"[10] on the theory that multiracial individuals "as a group may be the embodiment of

America's best chance to clean up race relations."[11] Indeed, the equating of racial mixture with racial harmony is often quite explicit. Harvard sociologist Orlando Patterson agrees: "If your object is the eventual integration of the races, a mixed-race or middle group is something you'd want to see developing. . . . The middle group grows larger and larger, and the races eventually blend."[12] Similarly, demographer William Frey, the author of "Diversity Explosion: How New Racial Demographics Are Remaking America," asserts that multiracial identity will blur racial divisions and soothe cultural tensions.[13] The multiracial discourse narrative thus posits that "mixing away" racism will absolve the nation from having to address entrenched racial disparities in socioeconomic opportunity.[14]

Yet, the current valorization of multiracial people is part of a complex dualism. This is the case because the imagining of mixed-race people as shamans of racial peace is accompanied by a social reality in which multiracial people are targets of racial discrimination. The idealization of Hawaii as a site of mixed-race racial harmony is a perfect example of this dualism. Sociologist Laura Desfor Edles notes that "the myth of Hawai'i as a model minority state grossly misconstrues the complex workings of racialization."[15] Overinvestment in the notion of Hawaii as an exceptional multiracial space has been accomplished by an ahistorical envisioning of Hawaii devoid of its realities of racial hierarchy and subordination within the midst of racial mixture. Hawaiians are thus imagined as mixed-race symbols of racial peace at the same time that their victimization as targets of discrimination is overlooked. It is thus prudent to treat with caution any celebrations of multiracial identity that attribute mystical healing and racial knowledge to mixed-race persons. Yet the public discourse is greatly animated by the idealization of multiracial people, as best exemplified by news stories such as that of the *New York Times*' "What Biracial People Know" article extolling the presumption that "multiracial people are more open-minded and creative."[16]

Indeed, the captivation with multiracial identity has also entered the antidiscrimination law legal context. Specifically, the presence of fluid mixed-race racial identities within allegations of discrimination leads some legal scholars to conclude that civil rights laws are in urgent need of reform because they were developed with a strictly binary foundation of blackness and whiteness. Building upon the social movement for recognition of multiracial identity on the census and generally, scholars conclude that courts misunderstand the nature of discrimination against mixed-race persons when they do not specifically acknowledge the distinctiveness of their multiracial identity. Even United States Supreme Court litigation has begun to associate the growth of multiracial identity with the obsolescence of civil rights policies. Particularly worrisome has been the judicial suggestion that the growth of multiracial identity undercuts the legitimacy of affirmative action policies that have long sought to pursue racial equality.

The supposition that the multiracial experience of discrimination is exceptional, and not well understood or handled by present antidiscrimination law, is evident in the publications of several multiracial-identity scholars. I coin the term "multiracial-identity scholars" to refer to authors whose scholarship promotes the recognition of the distinct challenges that multiracial identity now presumably presents for civil rights law.[17] For instance, the central claim in legal scholar Nancy Leong's much-cited article "Judicial Erasure of Mixed-Race Discrimination"[18] is that mixed-race discrimination claims are not properly administered by the legal system because the mixed-race specificity of the claims is ignored. Other legal scholars agree with Leong's assessment. Taking up Leong's analysis, Scot Rives and Tina Fernandes each in turn assert that the legal system is unable to address the "unique harms" of multiracial complaints without a specific "multiracial category" in antidiscrimination jurisprudence.[19] In turn, Leora Eisenstadt includes multiracial identity within her call for the creation of a concept of "fluid identity discrimination" where antidiscrimination statutes recognize the fluid nature of identity.[20] Similarly, Camille Gear Rich contends that fluid multiracial claims present "special challenges for antidiscrimination law."[21] Each of these reform proposals will be discussed further in the next section of this chapter and later in chapter 6.

Before evaluating the varied proposals that the multiracial-identity scholars set forth, it is important to note that they raise an important point—as interracial couples and multiracial identities proliferate, is a civil rights structure born in black-white binaries sufficient? Is it commodious enough to address the increasing fluidity of racial identity in a changing society? How does or should the move to multiple category checking on the census change the enforcement of civil rights law? This book will explore these questions, with an eye toward determining whether current law is sufficient to meet the intended goal of these laws, which is to address and rectify discrimination in public spheres.

The crux of the multiracial-identity-scholar critique of the emerging cases is that courts often reframe multiracial complainants' self-identities by describing mixed-race complainants as "monoracial" minority individuals.[22] Specifically, in many cases, judges refer to mixed-race claimants as solely African American or black.[23] These scholars take issue with this characterization, arguing that it hinders the recognition of the racial discrimination that multiracial individuals experience.

In order to examine the important questions that the multiracial-identity scholars raise, *Multiracials and Civil Rights* conducts a rigorous review of the early cases that the scholars refer to, and a larger pool of cases that arose after their publications were released. In addition, this book goes beyond the workplace-discrimination context that the multiracial-identity scholars have focused upon, and instead extends into antidiscrimination law enforcement in education, housing, public accommodations, and criminal justice. My close examination of the larger body of claims illuminates a disjuncture between the multiracial-identity scholars' theoretical critique of antidiscrimination law and the actual adequacy of the judicial administration of the claims.

Specifically, in an overwhelming number of the cases the scholars rely upon, the facts present a complainant whose description of the alleged discrimination includes pointed and derogatory comments about non-whiteness, and blackness in particular. The overarching commonality in the cases is the exceptionalism of nonwhiteness and blackness, rather than multiraciality, as subject to victimization. Although the claimants may personally identify as multiracial persons, they present allegations of public discrimination rooted in a bias against nonwhiteness that is not novel or particular to mixed-race persons, nor especially difficult for judges to understand. Particularly noteworthy is the fact that it is multiracials of African ancestry who overwhelmingly file multiracial-identified racial-discrimination legal claims, despite the fact that only 7.4 percent of blacks selected more than one race on the 2010 Census and only 4.8 percent did so on the 2000 Census.[24]

The Pew Research Center estimates that it is Native Americans with white ancestry who represent the largest proportion of the U.S. multiracial population, comprising 50 percent of all multiracials (when the racial identities of parents and grandparents are the sole considerations),[25] and that Native Hawaiians and other Pacific Islanders were the group with the highest proportion of its members selecting multiple races on the 2010 and 2000 censuses (at a rate of 55.9 percent and 54.4 percent, respectively).[26] Yet black multiracials file the vast majority of discrimination claims. The absence of a broader representation of racial mixture in the universe of discrimination claims suggests that racial mixture itself is not the driving force of the discrimination alleged.

Moreover, the increase in the number of individuals identifying as mixed-race or multiracial does not present unique challenges to the pursuit of political equality inasmuch as the cases are mired in a long-existing morass of bias against nonwhiteness and its intimate connection to white dominance. Rather than point to a need for a shift away from the existing civil rights laws, the cases instead indicate the need for further support of the current structures. This book concludes that the multiracial discrimination cases are helpful in highlighting the continued need for attention to white supremacy and for fortifying the focus of civil rights law on racial privilege and the lingering legacy of bias against nonwhites.

The objective of the book is to elucidate the distinction between the presumed exceptional space that multiracial persons are rhetorically imagined to occupy in the public discourse and the binary nonwhite/white racial realties that they actually experience. By demonstrating the key difference between the reality of the cases and the theorized notions about the cases, *Multiracials and Civil Rights* seeks to further racial justice efforts by setting forth an overt "socio-political race" lens for analyzing matters of discrimination, rather than the personal racial identity perspective utilized by multiracial-identity scholars and legal actors. The socio-political race perspective meaningfully preserves an individual's ability to assert a varied personal identity, while providing a more effective tool for publicly addressing racism and pursuing equality.

Importantly, the book will illustrate that the claim for multiracial exceptionalism is deeply flawed, misses the continuing power of white dominance, and poses a real danger to equality. This will be done by tracing the legal challenges to race-based affirmative action over the last ten years and noting the ways in which Supreme Court affirmative action litigation has positioned mixed-race persons as disrupting the societal need for racial remediation. The empirical documentation of the book's cases disrupts this notion and shows that multiracials are not an exception to the white/nonwhite dynamic of racism and instead are being invoked as a tool to dismantle the protections of civil rights law.

In sum, the book will explore the following questions: (1) Does the increase in the number of individuals who identify as mixed-race present unique challenges to the pursuit of political equality? (2) How should law respond to multiracial racial identity in a manner that enables such persons to protect themselves from domination? and (3) Does the advent of multiracial racial identity necessitate a new vision of what racial equality means?

The exploration of these questions is grounded in an examination of all electronically available antidiscrimination law cases with mixed-race-identified claimants, within the discrimination contexts of employment, education, housing, public accommodations, and criminal justice. These contexts were specifically chosen because they form the bedrock of civil rights equality law. (The voting rights context was omitted because under the Voting Rights Act a group cannot raise a claim unless the group is sufficiently numerous and geographically compact to constitute a politically cohesive insular minority group in any given electoral unit.[27] Thus far, multiracials are too geographically dispersed to satisfy this criterion.) The cases were collected from the electronic case law databases of Westlaw and Lexis by seeking out each instance in which a claimant alleged racial discrimination and identified as "multiracial," "biracial," "mixed-race," "racially mixed" and "mixed-heritage." Excluded from the analysis were cases where a claimant happened to have mixed-race ancestry but did not personally identify as mixed-race, as the purpose of the inquiry is to explore the adequacy of the law's response to explicit multiracial identity. Thus, a case where a claimant raised a concern with discrimination because an employer exposed the "racial secret" of his black ancestry and thereby disrupted his self-representation as a "white" person was excluded because the claimant did not assert a specific multiracial identity.[28]

It should be noted that the compilation of cases includes the very same cases discussed by the multiracial-identity literature but greatly expands both their number and scope. While the multiracial-identity literature is primarily restricted to the discussion of eight employment-discrimination cases, my empirical study includes twenty-five employment court cases along with twelve additional administrative claims dealt with directly by the Equal Employment Opportunity Commission government agency. More importantly, this book extends beyond the multiracial-identity-literature sphere of the workplace, with an interrogation of claims regarding discrimination in education, housing, public accommodations, and the administration of criminal justice. Each of the aforementioned chapters directly engages the details of every relevant case in order to concretely demonstrate how the cases counter the multiracial-identity-scholar thesis of the inadequacy of antidiscrimination law. Given the deep-seated attachment to the notion that multiracial discrimination is a unique phenomenon that current antidiscrimination law is too narrow to properly address, it is especially important to be methodical and exacting in exposing the overwhelming number of cases that demonstrate the contrary. The stories that multiracial claimants themselves tell of their experiences of discrimination are at the heart of this book and its concern with eradicating racism for all.

Each of the chapter reviews of cases will discuss the relevant civil rights statutes and any parallel constitutional inequality claims that were raised by the claimants. The discussion of the cases begins with chapter 2's examination of the workplace context, the arena in which the greatest number of multiracial discrimination cases are filed. Chapter 3 will then assess educational discrimination claims. Chapter 4 will examine housing and public accommodations discrimination. Chapter 5 will consider the treatment of multiracials in the criminal justice system.

Chapter 6 will then unpack how despite the fact that the empirical record does not by and large show anti-mixture animus, what fundamentally concerns multiracial-identity scholars is the pursuit of "Personal Racial Identity Equality." The chapter will also examine the ill effects on antidiscrimination law of the multiracial "Personal Racial Identity Equality" approach to civil rights as evidenced by the rhetorical positioning of multiracials as the justification for dismantling affirmative action programs. Chapter 7 concludes by offering a socio-political race perspective on race to supplant the multiracial personal identity approach for assessing multiracial discrimination claims.

An Introduction to Antidiscrimination Law and Its Perceived Multiracial Failings

The chapters that follow will each describe discrimination allegations filed by multiracial claimants in a variety of legal contexts that include employment, education, housing, public accommodations, and criminal justice. While each of those areas has its own developed body of law, the equality principles that ground how to prove a claim of discrimination are based in several common precepts that it will be useful to introduce from the start for readers unfamiliar with this legal terrain.

Above all, the law understands discrimination as an unjustified difference in treatment informed by specifically prohibited considerations (such as race or gender) that causes harm. Not all human differences are protected by law from discrimination. For instance, some people may have more favorable views of tall as opposed to short persons, but antidiscrimination law does not cover height bias. Courts refer to those traits that are protected by law as "protected classes" or "protected groups."

Race is a protected category, and a person of any race can bring a claim of discrimination. In examining whether a claimant has proven that discrimination occurred, a court conducts an inquiry into what was done and how the claimant was adversely treated because of his or her racial difference. To articulate a coherent claim, it is thus mandatory to overtly assert that race was the prohibited category that influenced the differential treatment. For that reason, it is necessary for the claimant to identify his or her race as the racial difference that motivated the ill treatment. However, this is not a litmus test of racial identity. It is a review of actions and their results.[29] Racial identity is relevant only inasmuch as it illuminates how it motivated the adverse treatment. Hence, specific racial categories are not listed in the text of any antidiscrimination law, nor do courts limit the law to particular racial groups. Moreover, the same standard of proof applies to all race discrimination claims regardless of what the claimant's racial identity is.[30]

Infused into the articulation and interpretation of antidiscrimination law statutes such as the Civil Rights Act of 1964 is the foundational equality perspective of the Fourteenth Amendment of the U.S. Constitution. Its literal mandate that state governments not deny any person the equal protection of the laws has been judicially interpreted to require the same treatment for persons who are deemed similarly situated.[31] To illustrate, this means that a state employer cannot intentionally treat employees with similar credentials and work experience differently when they apply for the same promotion simply because they are of a different race.

The prohibition against states using racial differences to harm individuals is so considerable that race is treated as a "suspect category" for which the court must apply a strict scrutiny standard of review. Under the strict scrutiny standard, a state policy challenged as a violation of equal protection requires the demonstration of a compelling government interest to authorize the policy's use of race. The absence of a compelling government interest justifying a state policy incorporating explicit considerations of race makes the policy unconstitutional and thus void. The foundational case illustrating the constitutional principle against discrimination is that of *Brown v. Board of Education*.[32] In striking down a government educational policy of racially segregated schooling that violated the equal protection of the laws, *Brown* ushered in a flurry of legislation attempting to dismantle all forms of Jim Crow segregation.

It is important to note that the civil rights legislation that followed *Brown* was and continues to be broader than the constitutional equal protection standard. While the Constitution only applies to discrimination by government entities, federal and state statutes encompass private individuals and organizations as well. Moreover, case law decisions have limited the Constitution to the prohibition of only "intentional" discrimination. In contrast, to better address concerns with systemic and structural racism, statutory law is free to encompass restrictions on racially neutral policies that have racially disproportionate statistical discriminatory effects.

Thus, statutory antidiscrimination law goes beyond the doctrinal limitations on constitutional law at the same time that it shares the same fundamental goal of seeking racial equality. While it is true that both the constitutional antidiscrimination cases and statutory laws were developed in response to our nation's entrenched history of Jim Crow racial segregation, the contours of the doctrine are broad and extend beyond the Jim Crow context. The texts of our statutes and case law are in no way limited to a black-white understanding of race. Instead, they allow for capacious ways of considering how harmful treatment is manifested "on the ground of or because of race or color."[33] For this reason, groups other than African Americans, such as Asian Americans, Latinos, and Native Americans, are able to use the very same legal protections against discrimination as African Americans.[34] The abstract and open-ended nature of the language of the laws means that judges have a central role in interpreting what discrimination means.[35]

Judges find that often the most persuasive articulation of racial discrimination is made when the claimant can specifically identify how persons of another race in similar circumstances were not exposed to the same adverse treatment as the claimant. Such a comparison to a similarly situated "comparator" not of the claimant's racial background is not required by law but is useful to courts in identifying the differential treatment. A similar analysis applies when women are compared to men in gender discrimination claims, or disabled persons are compared to able-bodied persons in disability discrimination claims. In short, antidiscrimination law inquires about race and racial categories because its concern is the prohibition against using race as a basis for harming people.

However, multiracial-identity scholars take issue with antidiscrimination law's traditional focus on racial categories. For instance, Nancy Leong asserts that the judicial referencing of multiracial claimants with monoracial terms is a "judicial erasure of multiracial discrimination"[36] that trivializes the uniqueness of the discrimination and "entrenches the crude [single-race] racial categories in our social consciousness, along with the stereotypes associated with those categories."[37] For this reason, Leong proposes that "we should aspire to a more fluid understanding of race, one that acknowledges animus directed against a person's perceived race without an attendant need to define that person's 'objective' racial identity or to place that person in a category."[38] For Leong, the law's consideration of racial categories in assessing discrimination claims is ultimately what is problematic. Her proposal for "judicial recognition of those who are discriminated against because they are perceived as multiracial" is based on the conclusion that a unique mixed-race animus is propelling the cases, and that our current antidiscrimination laws are ill-equipped to navigate the terrain of perceived race.[39] Leora Eisenstadt adopts Leong's anticategory analysis to propose that antidiscrimination statutes like Title VII be amended "to explicitly recognize the fluid nature of identity" by adding protection based on "an individual's actual or perceived racial identity."[40]

Yet the shift to a "perceived race" regime will not be very helpful to multiracial discrimination victims like Cleon, whose story introduced this chapter. Cleon looked white, and thus his perceived race was white. The discriminatory treatment he received was not based on his perceived race but was instead motivated by the nonwhite results of his Ancestry. com test. Pointedly, the racial harassment all centered on the blackness revealed by his genetic test. Once Cleon was read by his workplace as tainted by blackness, his white appearance was immaterial. In other words, the racial category drove discrimination, not Cleon's appearance. Thus, for Cleon and many others whose appearance does not announce their racial ancestry, the anticategory approach to discrimination law will leave them without legal protection when others react with adverse treatment to the disclosure of nonwhite ancestry.[41] Legal scholar Angela Onwuachi-Willig describes a similar shortcoming for white-appearing individuals who begin to experience racial discrimination when it is revealed that they have a nonwhite partner and/or nonwhite children.[42]

Rather than denounce the antidiscrimination law concept of racial categories outright, other multiracial-identity scholars instead advocate for the insertion of a multiracial category into the legal doctrine. For example, Scot Rives and Tina Fernandes agree with Nancy Leong's assessment about the inadequacy of the racial category approach, but both prefer that an explicit "multiracial" category be inserted into the legal doctrine.[43] However, as previously noted, antidiscrimination law is not designed with specific racial categories. As the chapters that follow will delineate, the laws are formulated according to whether an individual of any race has been treated differently than someone of a different race. The laws do not specify particular races for inclusion and enforcement. Nevertheless, Scot Rives asserts that a "separate category for mixed race is necessary to redress the unique harms targeting mixed-race persons,"[44] and Tina Fernandes proposes that constitutional equal protection doctrine specify that multiracial persons be treated as a suspect class distinct from the existing suspect class of "race" and that statutory civil rights law "add Multiracial to the list of available racial identities."[45]

Furthermore, Fernandes also recommends that government agencies receiving discrimination complaints add a multiracial category to their intake questionnaires, in lieu of the current format of inviting respondents to designate multiple races as they like.[46] Such questionnaires are not mandated by civil rights law and exist simply to streamline the process of filing a claim for a government agency to investigate.[47] The current questionnaires like the decennial census permit a respondent to indicate multiple racial ancestries, and to attach additional pages to describe the discrimination allegations.

Since antidiscrimination law already permits claimants to describe their racial identity however they choose as long as they are alleging that some act of discrimination was "because of race," it is puzzling why Rives and Fernandes insist that statutes be amended to specifically include a multiracial category. No other racial identity is expressly written into the statutory texts. There is no Asian-specific antidiscrimination law or Latino-specific antidiscrimination law. Nor have Asian and Latino civil rights organizations using the existing laws to protect their constituents from discrimination (such as the Asian American Legal Defense Fund, Latino Justice, or the Mexican American Legal Defense Fund) argued that there should be.

Given the incoherence of demanding the insertion of a multiracial category where no other racial categories are statutorily specified, it is particularly troubling that the rhetoric of multiracial exceptionality that is used for the demand is being drawn upon by the Supreme Court to question the need for policies of racial inclusion. Simply stated, theorizing that multiracials require exceptional treatment from antidiscrimination law bolsters harmful attempts to dismantle the civil rights laws that currently exist. Thus, despite the differences in specific law reform proposals made by the multiracial-identity scholars, they are united in their presumption that mixed-race personal identity necessitates a change to civil rights law in ways that actually endanger the ability to protect multiracials and others from discrimination. This book seeks to provide a corrective to such a course.

2

Multiracial Employment Discrimination

> This is precisely the point: the racial mixture takes place
> within the context of social inequality. Amid all the glorifica-
> tion of mixture, some mixtures are more valued than others.
> —Miriam Jiménez Román, *A Companion to Latina/o Studies*[1]

Jill Mitchell is a light-skinned biracial woman with a black father and
white mother. On the basis of her appearance, many people presume she
is of mixed Hispanic and European descent. Mitchell started working
for Champs Sports in Beaumont, Texas, in 1996 as a full-time management trainee. She worked for a year without incident and received praise
about her work performance. But she felt her entire work experience
changed once her store manager discovered that her racial background
included African ancestry despite the fact that Mitchell did not disclose
her race on her job application and declined to identify her racial background when asked during the job interview. The manager deduced
Mitchell's racial background from the repeated visits to the store from
her darker-skinned relatives and friends.

Mitchell says the manager's "attitude towards her changed dramati-
cally" as he fixated on her African ancestry.[2] He often made negative
remarks about blacks to Mitchell and, on one occasion, remarked to
Mitchell that "she only dated black men"[3] as if that were problematic. At
one point Mitchell overheard the manager state, "We need to get her out
of here." The store manager's racialized treatment of Mitchell continued
until she was eventually demoted, and her former position was filled
with a white employee who came not from the ranks of the established
management trainee program like herself but instead from the part-time
hires.[4] As a result, she attributed her demotion to race discrimination

and filed an employment discrimination claim pursuant to Title VII of the Civil Rights Act of 1964.[5]

Jill Mitchell's chances for winning her lawsuit were quite low. This was the case not because of the relative merits of her claim but because it has been empirically documented that few complaints of racial discrimination ever yield success for claimants.[6] The vast majority of racial discrimination claims are dismissed by courts without the opportunity for a trial. For instance, from 1979 through 2006, federal claimants only won 15 percent of job-discrimination cases. By comparison, in all other civil cases, the win rate was 51 percent.[7] Commentators attribute the low success rate to the growing hostility with which courts approach allegations of discrimination.[8] Courts seemingly believe that the passage of civil rights laws alone has wrought a postracial society in which instances of discrimination are rare.

Despite the overarching challenge of persuading courts that an instance of discrimination had actually occurred, Jill Mitchell's motion for court-appointed counsel was granted, with the court noting that "the merits of Mitchell's allegations weigh in favor of granting the motion."[9] While the published opinion does not entail a substantive resolution of the discrimination charge, it is still quite a victory in the context of contemporary judicial animosity to any discrimination claim.[10] Here the court simultaneously endorses the merits of the claim of discrimination and authorizes the funds for a court-appointed lawyer. Court-appointed counsel is only mandatory in criminal cases where a defendant's liberty is at stake. It is thus remarkable that the judge authorized a court-appointed lawyer in this employment discrimination case.

Having a lawyer represent the claimant is a huge advantage in that the claim will be professionally researched for the most persuasive articulation of the case's merits. This also provides a more level playing field in a context where nearly all employers have the resources to retain attorneys. Indeed, it seems likely from the record that a confidential settlement agreement was reached in the case after Mitchell obtained a court-appointed lawyer. The implication of a confidential settlement agreement is suggested by the claimant's choice to request that the lawsuit be dismissed with prejudice rather than proceed with a judicial inquiry.

What then do multiracial-identity scholars find problematic about the judicial administration of this biracial-identified claimant's case? Throughout the opinion, the court refers to Mitchell as "black."[11] For the multiracial-identity scholars, the court's singular focus on blackness means that despite the favorable outcome, the court failed to recognize the possibility that Mitchell's mistreatment was the product of anti-multiracial bias.[12] From their perspective, the court's oversimplified reference to Mitchell as black is analytically problematic despite the fact that the court also emphatically states that Mitchell has a discrimination claim that should proceed and warrants the dedication of public resources in a court-appointed attorney.

More importantly, the court's oversimplification of the claimant's racial identity in court documents parallels the singular salience of blackness that Mitchell's own narrative raises. Nor can the black focus of her own factual allegations be dismissed as the strategic coaching of an attorney seeking to situate the case within the traditional paradigm of white versus black racism, because Mitchell represented herself, and the black-focused narrative appeared in her own testimony before the magistrate judge in her hearing to request court-appointed counsel. In fact, 39 percent of the multiracial workplace discrimination cases assessed in this chapter were filed by complainants representing themselves and using their own words to describe how they felt targeted and harmed. Thus, the recurrent theme of the primacy of bias against nonwhiteness and anti-blackness specifically is not the artificial imposition of a lawyer's strategic construct. The *Mitchell* case then is inappropriately labeled by multiracial-identity scholars as illustrating a judicial confusion about the nature of multiracial discrimination or the inadequacy of the existing antidiscrimination legal framework. Instead, the *Mitchell* case demonstrates the coherence of judicially focusing on blackness when the claimant articulates a factual pattern enmeshed in anti-black bias.

Multiracial Discrimination within Overarching Nonwhite Discrimination

As in Jill Mitchell's case, the vast majority of multiracial stories of discrimination entail allegations of nonwhite or specifically anti-black bias rather than prejudice rooted in hostility towards racial mixture itself.[13] Indeed, many more cases implicate anti-black bias than any other form of racial discrimination. This pattern is particularly striking within the context of workplace discrimination claims filed in federal courts pursuant to the Civil Rights Act of 1964's prohibition against employment discrimination. This chapter's analysis is based upon an examination of all the relevant cases made available in the electronic databases of Westlaw and Lexis.[14] The cases include all those discussed by multiracial-identity scholars, but the chapter goes beyond that small cluster to encompass more recent cases.

Eighty-eight percent of these published employment cases (twenty-two out of twenty-five) involved claimants with African ancestry in their mixture, while only 12 percent (three out of twenty-five) involved non-black multiracial claimants. This predominance of black ancestry as an animating factor of the discrimination is also evident in cases excluded from analysis because the claimants failed to file their claims by the statutory deadline for court consideration.[15] But this pattern of black ancestry is seemingly viewed as inconsequential by the multiracial-identity scholars, who instead emphasize what they view as the problematic judicial focus on "monoracial" blackness rather than the mixed-race complexity of the complainant's personal identity.[16] What their critique underemphasizes is the significance of public anti-black bias. This insight is overlooked by multiracial-identity scholars even in cases where multiracial claimants experience outright success with their cases. Marlon Hattimore's case in *Richmond v. General Nutrition Centers, Inc.*[17] serves as a prime example.

Marlon Hattimore was hired as a sales associate in 2004 for GNC (General Nutrition Center) in its Newburgh, New York, store. After Hattimore was hired, the regional manager visited the store and upon seeing Hattimore he told the store manager that too many black people worked in the store and that Hattimore should thus be fired. Only after the regional manager was informed that Hattimore was biracial did he desist from firing Hattimore and begin to treat him with greater civility.

Hattimore was eventually assigned to work at a different GNC store and promoted to a store manager position.[18] However, while Hattimore's biracial status somewhat insulated him from the regional manager's hostility against black people as a group, Hattimore was still paid less than two subordinate, less experienced white employees.[19] Indeed, during his two-year tenure as a store manager, Hattimore endured a relentless pattern of hearing racially charged statements from the regional manager.[20] For instance, the regional manager referred to another employee who was black as "ghetto black trash" and remarked, "You can't take a hoodlum and put him in a business suit."[21] Hattimore also indicated that the regional manager compelled him to terminate a black employee by threatening to fire Hattimore if he did not comply.[22] Finally, Hattimore claimed he was terminated and replaced by a white individual and that the regional manager and GNC headquarters refused to tell him the reason he was fired.[23]

Hattimore then decided to join three other GNC employees in filing a joint lawsuit for racial discrimination. Hattimore's three co-claimants identified as black men from Jamaica and Ghana. GNC requested that the claims be dismissed outright on a motion for summary judgment. (A summary judgment is a pre-verdict judgment rendered by a court after a party shows that the absence of a factual dispute on one or more of the issues eliminates the need to send those issues to a trial and instead allows for the case to be promptly decided by the judge solely on the questions of law.)[24] The court denied GNC's petition to have the disparate-pay and discriminatory-termination claims dismissed outright.[25] Here the judge denied the motion due to evidence in the record of unequal pay and the existence of a factual dispute as to whether the claimant was officially terminated. A court's denial of a defendant's motion for summary judgment suggests that "a judge has given quasi-approval to the complainant's case," and thus often results in an employer's offer of favorable settlement for an employee, as it did in this case when the case later settled.[26] Furthermore, simply having a racial discrimination case "survive" employer requests for dismissal before a trial is scheduled is a victory in and of itself given the phenomenon of disproportionate early dismissal of vast numbers of racial discrimination cases across the country.

Nevertheless, the significance of this legal victory for Hattimore is lost in the multiracial-identity-scholar concern with the lack of a judicial elaboration of mixed-race identity. For the multiracial-identity scholars, Hattimore's case represents yet another court again treating a biracial claimant with African ancestry as solely black. However, the court's references to Hattimore as being in the targeted group of blacks did not harm his case because Hattimore presented a claim about being treated poorly because of his black ancestry, not because he is biracial. In fact, his biracial status was at times a mitigating factor in the discrimination against workers the regional manager identified as simply "black." More importantly, GNC was a workplace where "whiteness" was rewarded and blackness was ultimately penalized in whatever proportion it was represented in an employee's ancestry. In turn, the court focused on the salience of blackness that the claimant himself articulated and viewed the claimant's allegations as warranting further judicial inquiry. Thereafter GNC reached a settlement with the claimant. This was a huge victory for Hattimore. The court treated his discrimination claim with respect, and Hattimore was able to resolve the dispute directly with an out-of-court settlement. Multiracial-identity scholars do not make clear how Hattimore's case would have benefited from the court treating Hattimore solely as biracial rather than as part of the group of black employees being discriminated against.

Courts also appropriately respond to a multiracial claimant's concern with discrimination even when they ultimately decide that the employer has successfully asserted a nondiscriminatory reason that explains its actions, or that the evidence is insufficient to sustain the claim.[27] This is evident in *Smith v. CA, Inc.*[28] In the case, Walter Smith, a "biracial African American and Caucasian," asserted that he was subjected to racially discriminatory treatment for the year he worked as a data and life cycle management telesales executive in Tampa, Florida, in 2005.[29] The court stated, "There is no dispute that Smith was a member of a protected group as a biracial African American and Caucasian," thereby confirming his right to file a race discrimination claim. But Smith was not successful because the isolated allegations of harassment in the claim were not sufficiently severe or pervasive "to alter the conditions of his employment"[30] as required by the legal standard for a hostile work environment claim.

As a legal matter, an employer can only be held liable for the racial harassment among coworkers if the employer was negligent in controlling the work conditions and responding to the internal complaints of harassment.[31] When a coworker referred to Smith as a "boy" and "bitch," the incident was investigated and the harassing coworker was terminated. When a picture of a blue fish that Smith considered racially discriminatory was hung near Smith's cubicle, his employer removed it. The court records do not explain why Smith considered the blue fish racially offensive. However, because Smith's employer appropriately responded to each instance of alleged racial harassment as it arose, the employer could not be legally faulted for sustaining a hostile work environment. *Smith* is an example of the legal demand for "severe and pervasive" instances of harassment necessary to sustain a hostile work environment claim that complainants of all races and genders are subjected to.[32] In other words, Smith's multiracial status was not an analytical complication for the court.

While Smith did allege that his employer classified him as African American in its records against his will, he did not elaborate how the employer's racial classification harmed him or altered the conditions of his employment. Smith was not demoted, terminated, or targeted for an adverse employment action based upon the employer's racial classification. Significantly, Smith conceded in court that he was frequently absent from work, and the court thus concluded that Smith was terminated for his failure to follow the established workplace policies with respect to attendance and requesting time off with notice.

It is thus curious that the multiracial-identity-scholar critique of the case is that "the court failed even to acknowledge that, were it to grapple with the sufficiency of Smith's allegations of discrimination, the question was a complicated one."[33] The argument is that "[b]y failing to engage the possibility that the [harassing] comments were motivated by the employer's identification of Smith as biracial rather than Black, the court essentially ignored the record evidence that potentially supported a reading of animus against Smith as biracial."[34] This conjecture, though, is divorced from the reality of burdensome evidence requirements imposed on all employment discrimination complainants across race and gender. Such legal standards discount the significance of isolated incidents of discriminatory commentary and expressions of bias.[35]

More importantly, the derogatory comments made at Smith's expense are rooted in anti-black rather than multiracial bias. Specifically, a coworker called Smith a "bitch" and a "boy."[36] These terms historically reflect anti-black bias.[37] "[I]ndeed, there is a long racial history of black men being called boys as a method to subordinate them by imbuing persons of their racial status as incapable of full human personhood."[38] On one occasion, Smith's supervisor made an offensive remark regarding Smith's paternity suit, disparaging African American fathers when he stated he was surprised that an African American father like Smith would fight so hard for custody of his children.[39] The multiracial-identity-scholar description of the remark as "ambiguous" because "it might have been motivated by animus against Black people, or it might have been targeted at Smith because he had a Black father and a White mother"[40] understates the extent to which the comment again directly implicates a societal pattern of anti-black bias with the stereotype of black men being absentee fathers.[41]

Indeed, many more multiracial claimant cases implicate anti-black bias than any other discrimination. For instance, in *Watkins v. Hospital-*

ity Group Management, Inc.,[42] mixed-race complainant Victoria Watkins alleged racial discrimination after she was terminated in 2001 from her position as assistant general manager at the Sleep Inn hotel in Greensboro, North Carolina, where her coworkers referred to her as black.[43] Because a white male with less experience filled Victoria's position after she was terminated, the court refused to dismiss the discrimination charge as requested by the employer and instead allowed the claim to proceed to a jury trial. Having a racial discrimination claim make it to the jury trial phase is a very rare occurrence in contemporary U.S. courts.[44] Once the case proceeded to trial, the jury was persuaded that the actual cause for Watkins's termination was her unexplained absence from work over the course of an entire week in September 2001.

Nevertheless, the multiracial-identity-scholar critique of the case is that the court "found it obvious that a mixed-race person was a member of a different racial class than a white person—so obvious, in fact, that no further analysis was needed."[45] The opposition is to the court simply stating that a mixed-race complainant belongs to a "racial minority."[46] It is argued that this practice "impl[ies] that minority membership is both obvious and self-defining."[47] More importantly, the conclusion is that this demonstrates yet another court's reluctance to tackle the complexity of mixed-race discrimination claims.[48]

However, the very legal issue that Victoria Watkins sought to have addressed was her employer's displacement of her in favor of a white employee not on the basis of her mixed-race status but solely because of the African ancestry in her mixture that contrasted with her white replacement. That was an invitation to the court to treat her mixed-race identity as different from whiteness in the way that it was allegedly viewed as distinctive in the workplace. In fact, rather than illustrate a court's reluctance to engage the complexity of multiracial discrimination claims, the case exemplifies a court accurately pinpointing the essence of the racial differentiation described by the claimant herself.

Victoria Watkins's personal mixed-race identity may be complex, but she did not assert that personal complexity as salient to her public experience of discrimination. Watkins's opposition was to being viewed as an inferior nonwhite other in comparison to whites. Criticizing the court for not engaging in a complexity that was neither raised by the complainant nor germane to the inquiry into discrimination seems misplaced. Indeed, the absence of a judicial elaboration of multiracial identity has not interfered with the judicial administration of multiracial claims like Watkins's. Moreover, a similar white versus nonwhite pattern of hostility is evident in the vast majority of multiracial discrimination cases.

Nor is the judicial receptivity to multiracial claims restricted to allegations of anti-black bias.[49] In *Doner-Hendrick v. New York Institute of Technology*,[50] Henrietta Doner-Hendrick, a multiracial Filipina American, brought a discrimination claim, which survived the employer's motion to dismiss.[51] In 2008 Doner-Hendrick taught computer graphics (CG) for the New York Institute of Technology at its campus in Amman, Jordan, under a three-year contract.[52] In April 2009, she reported to her superior that she observed Catherine Kourouklis, a Caucasian faculty member who was the coordinator of the CG department, "scold and explicitly insult another professor for his devotion to Islam."[53] Although Kourouklis was replaced as the coordinator of the CG department, she was allowed to remain on the faculty.[54]

In contrast, Doner-Hendrick was terminated midway through her three-year contract, in November 2009, after making what the court described as "a religiously provocative—though not clearly inappropriate—comment" to her class.[55] Doner-Hendrick, hoping to promote creative thinking among her students, asked that they create a "shoe-shaped pink mosque that would be for women only."[56] The court found an inference of race discrimination could be drawn from Doner-Hendrick's termination because Kouroulis, a Caucasian, was treated more favorably by being allowed to remain on the faculty after her demonstration of explicit religious intolerance, while Doner-Hendrick, who is Filipina, was terminated for her implicit critique of Islam.[57]

Thus the court's analysis of the racial discrimination as bounded by a white versus nonwhite reality responded to Doner-Hendrick's own factual allegations of a white versus nonwhite racial binary treatment in the workplace. In fact, after the court refused to dismiss the case and thus validated the viability of the claim, the parties successfully entered into a confidential settlement agreement.[58] Thus *Doner-Hendrick* illustrates the parallels of one of the very few non-black-related multiracial claims with the universe of cases deeply embedded in patterns of nonwhite bias. Notwithstanding the existence of *Doner-Hendrick* as a non-black-related multiracial discrimination case, multiracial-identity scholars are primarily concerned with what they view as a judicial overemphasis on blackness.

In addition to the multiracial-identity-scholar concern with courts that seemingly overemphasize blackness and nonwhiteness in the claims of multiracial claimants, they also take issue with the judicial method for analyzing the cases. This is the concern regarding the racial groups to which multiracial claimants are judicially compared in order to assess whether there has been differential treatment based on race. The actual texts of antidiscrimination laws do not mandate that discrimination be proved only by showing that members of other races similarly situated to the complainant were treated better than the complainant solely because of race. Nevertheless, the judicial search for such a "comparator [to] make discrimination visible with the occurrence of comparatively adverse treatment . . . has emerged as the predominant methodological device for evaluating discrimination claims."[59]

In the multiracial-identity-scholar assessment, the judicial demand for a comparator can be especially onerous for multiracial complainants, who "do not squarely fit into familiar racial categories."[60] Unfortunately, the judicial demand for comparator evidence (of a different-race person to compare the complainant to who has not experienced discrimination from the same actor) has been documented to be problematic in even nonmultiracial "run-of-the-mill cases" where comparisons to employees with different supervisors or with insufficiently similar job responsibilities are viewed as inadequate for proving discrimination by comparison.[61] The challenge of locating comparators similarly situated to the complainant in all material respects is not unique to multiracial complainants or particularly more onerous for them to deal with. In fact, the majority of multiracial complainants have narratives that invite a comparison to white coworkers in much the same way most other nonwhite complainants do.

For instance, in the 2011 case of *Doyle v. Denver Dep't of Human Services*,[62] Celeste Doyle, a biracial African American and Hispanic probationary employee, brought hostile work environment and race discrimination claims against her former employer, Denver Department of Human Services (DDHS).[63] Doyle provided evidence of numerous racial incidents and remarks made by her coworkers.[64] Such comments included a coworker's remark that DDHS only hires "monkeys and niggers."[65] This same coworker drew an offensive picture of Doyle, in which he depicted stereotypical physical features of African Americans by accentuating her lips and nose.[66] Other coworkers referred to Doyle as "nigger," "Hispanigger," and "spic" during a conversation they had in front of Doyle.[67]

These incidents reflect bias against nonwhites and not anti-mixture bias per se. As a result, the court sought evidence of anti-white discrimination in the workplace and concluded that Doyle failed to "show that similarly situated non-minority employees were treated more favorably."[68] This is the case because two of Doyle's white coworkers were also probationary employees and were fired near the time of her termination.[69] Using those two white employees as "comparators" to compare to Doyle's own dismissal undermined for the court the allegation that Doyle's parallel dismissal as a probationary employee was somehow the result of discrimination.

For a court using the comparator approach for evaluating discrimination claims, the parallel treatment of employees across racial groups with similar employment status obviates the need for further inquiry. This of course overlooks the possibility that racial bias could have motivated the dismissal of a nonwhite employee at the same time that other white employees were terminated for other reasons. Thus it is appropriate to criticize the constraints of the comparator approach for assessing discrimination claims. But the limitations of the comparator analysis are not particular to multiracial claimants. All racial minorities are hindered in their claims of discrimination when a similarly situated white employee suffers the same employment outcome they do. Nor did the *Doyle* court struggle to identify relevant comparators because of Doyle's multiracial status. Thus despite the fact that the *Doyle* race discrimination claim failed, the case demonstrates that the comparator approach is not uniquely problematic for multiracial claimants.

In fact, in contrast to the comparator analysis constraints on the discriminatory dismissal allegation, Doyle's hostile work environment racial harassment claim was deemed a viable claim by the judge and allowed to proceed to trial. After a seven-day jury trial in which Doyle failed to present any former or current employees to testify regarding her allegation of a hostile work environment, and during which the employer's lawyer portrayed Doyle as a liar after questioning her about a ten-year-old felony conviction for attempting to pass ten thousand dollars in counterfeit money at a casino, the jury did not find Doyle's allegations believable. With the employer's characterization of Doyle as being tantamount to an unrepentant liar, the absence of any witnesses to support her story was detrimental to her case. While unfortunate for Doyle, the outcome of the case was not complicated by her multiracial identity.

In only one case dating back to 1994 has a judge categorically objected to limiting the comparator analysis to a white versus nonwhite comparison.[70] In the case of *Walker v. Colorado*, George Walker identified himself as a "multiracial person of Black, Native American, Jewish and Anglo descent" and alleged that he was not hired as associate vice president of human resources and personnel at the University of Colorado because of his race. But rather than limit its inquiry to how "multiracial persons" were differentially treated, as Walker requested, the court decided that "multiracial persons may be considered members of each of the protected groups with which they have any significant identification."[71] This was the case because the court was concerned that a singular class of multiracial persons "would be impracticable to apply and could be so self-limiting that a particular person is the only identifiable member of the group."[72]

The multiracial-identity-scholar assessment of *Walker* expresses concern that the complainant's claim would too easily be defeated if the individual hired was considered a member of any of the groups making up the multiracial person's identity. The concern is that simultaneously counting a multiracial claimant as a member of many other racial groups in the workplace would leave the complainant with few to no other groups to compare his or her treatment to. Hence only if an employee of Walker's same qualifications who was not either black, Native American, Jewish, or white was treated better than Walker under similar circumstances could Walker establish a claim of discriminatory treatment. Yet the court in *Walker* was careful to note that the fact that a "black" person was selected instead of the complainant would not, in itself, defeat his claim. Indeed, the case was ultimately dismissed not because of the court's chosen comparator assessment but instead because the university had limited applications to current employees (unlike Walker) for administrative reasons deemed nondiscriminatory.

Nevertheless, the language of the *Walker* court so limiting the comparator analysis for multiracial complainants would be troubling if not mitigated by the court's subsequent proceedings. In 2007, Walker applied for another position with the University of Colorado, that of president of the university. When Walker again identified himself as "a man of Anglo, Black, Jewish and Native American Indian ancestry," the court executed a dramatic reversal by noting that on the basis of the claimant's racial identity, "there is no dispute that Plaintiff [the complainant] belongs to a protected class."[73] Indeed, the court noted the analytical relevance of the employer having rejected Walker in favor of a "Caucasian" candidate.[74] Only when Walker failed to provide evidence that he met the stated qualifications for the position of university president was his claim dismissed.

Thus, the one aberrant case harshly restricting the ability of a multiracial claimant to prove discrimination has been seemingly overruled by the subsequent analysis of the same court. Why the shift in the sixteen years between the 1994 and 2010 court decisions? Perhaps with the greater dissemination of information about multiracial identity and mixed-race public figures like President Obama, the court was better able to situate multiracial identity as a nonwhite identity equally subject to the harms of nonwhite bias and racial hierarchy. The unmitigating anti-black invectives President Obama was subjected to during his presidency certainly situated multiracial status as part of the societal dynamic of bias against nonwhiteness. When viewed in the continuum of white supremacy, the racial position of multiracial status is not so difficult to discern. This is just as salient in cases where no self-identified whites are present but whiteness is at issue nonetheless. As the next section discusses, white privilege can also be attributed to multiracial persons.

Multiracial Discrimination within African American Race and Color Discrimination

The few cases in which the factual allegations more closely approximate a concern with racial mixture itself arise when self-identified African American coworkers and supervisors are alleged to have expressed race and skin-color bias. But far from raising novel claims, the factual allegations follow a historically familiar pattern of dark-skinned African Americans acting in a retaliatory fashion towards light-skinned persons they fear bear attitudes of superiority for how closely their skin or phenotype approximates whiteness.[75] While mixture is presumed to generate the light skin tone, lightness itself, rather than mixture alone, seemingly causes the workplace hostility.

Like longstanding color discrimination claims among African Americans who do not identify as multiracial (as with the many African Americans whose light skin tone is not the result of interracial marriage but the legacy of the sexual violence under slavery), the contemporary multiracial claims regarding African American agents of discrimination are rooted in historical anxiety.[76] Specifically, the concern is that the resemblance to whiteness will be accompanied by color bias, which has been an unfortunate part of the African American community. The point here is not that these cases are any less vexing due to their connections to preexisting color discrimination bias, but rather that they are not brand-new forms of discrimination necessitating presumably "multiracial" legal reforms.

In fact, in contrast to many of the explicitly intraracial African American versus African American color discrimination claims, courts have been even more receptive to multiracial versus African American colorism claims.[77] Notably, the very first court case to recognize the claim of color-based employment discrimination under the Civil Rights Act of 1964 was one in which the claimant was a light-skinned mixed-race employee alleging bias on the part of her darker-skinned African American supervisor.[78] The decision is even more remarkable when one considers that the vast majority of color-based claims are filed by dark-skinned employees aggrieved by the discrimination of their lighter-skinned supervisors in ways that track all the social science research documenting the penalty that dark skin imposes in the labor market and most other sectors.[79]

For instance, dark skin tone has been documented to often be more determinative of hiring practices for African Americans than academic credentials.[80] When presented with prospective employee profiles that differ only by the skin color portrayed in a photograph, respondents show a preference for lighter-skinned candidates for employment.[81] A light-skinned black male can have only a bachelor's degree and entry-level work experience and still be preferred over a dark-skinned black male with an MBA and past managerial positions, simply because expectations of the light-skinned black male are much higher, and he does not appear as "menacing" as the darker-skinned male applicant.[82] This same dynamic is reflected in sentencing outcomes for dark-skinned first-time offenders, who receive longer sentences for the same crimes that lighter-skinned black offenders commit.[83]

The preference for lighter-skinned African Americans is also exhibited in the hiring practices for actors in films and advertisements, television news personnel, and tenure-track university professors.[84] Light-skin color preferences have also been documented in immigrant workforce hiring patterns.[85] In addition to employee selection, color biases also manifest themselves in the allocation of wages.[86] In fact, some studies indicate that darker-skinned labor force participants are more prone to experiencing employment discrimination than lighter-skinned workers.[87]

Importantly, the few existing multiracial cases rooted in skin-color bias evince coherent judicial analyses that appropriately administer the claims. For instance, in the 2011 case of *Graves v. District of Columbia*,[88] Stephen Graves, a mixed-race employee of "Native American, African American, and Caucasian heritage," brought a hostile work environment claim against the District of Columbia Fire and Emergency Services Department.[89] Graves described about eighty-one racially charged incidents that took place during his two-decade employment history.[90] Graves alleged that African American coworkers subjected him to the following derogatory comments and discriminatory incidents that took issue with his light skin as a racially mixed man of African ancestry. Graves was called "High Yellow," "Light Brown Wanna-be White," "White Boy," and "Red."[91] He was told, "[Y]ou think you're too good to be black" and "That's no way for a Black man to look."[92] A fire chief disparaged Graves for being friends with white employees.[93] Coworkers repeatedly commented on "the color of [Graves's] skin, eyes and hair."[94] A battalion fire chief told Graves that people disliked him because of his skin color and that he "would not have problems" if he were dark-skinned.[95] Graves claimed that a workplace equal employment opportunity officer refused to help him deal with the harassment because Graves "was in with 'the white boys.'"[96]

During another incident, Graves told a firefighter he could not wash his car at the fire station while off-duty.[97] The firefighter responded, "Fuck you faggot mother fucker, fucking white bitch can't tell me shit," and then spat in Graves's face.[98] In addition, an emergency medical technician inquired about "the authenticity of Graves' African American heritage" and "verbal abuse" culminated in her slapping Graves across the face.[99]

Yet none of these allegations caused the court confusion. When the employer attempted to have the case dismissed on a motion for summary judgment (with the assertion that the absence of a factual dispute eliminates the need to send those issues to a trial and that the question of law can be clearly resolved immediately by the judge), the court denied the motion.[100] The judge denied the motion for summary judgment because he concluded that issues as to whether the racial harassment was severe and pervasive were in question. The denial of such a motion indicates the court's conviction that the complainant's allegations are not frivolous.[101] Indeed, after the denial of a defendant's motion for summary judgment, many parties reach a settlement agreement. In *Graves*, the case proceeded to a jury trial and Graves was awarded fifty thousand dollars in compensation. Nor is *Graves* the only multiracial colorism claim with a successful resolution for the claimant.[102]

Even in cases where the court has ultimately ruled that the complainant's evidence is not strong enough, it has done so after making a substantive inquiry into the colorism allegations. For instance, in the 2009 case of *Kendall v. Urban League of Flint*,[103] biracial complainant Jamie Kendall brought a race discrimination claim, alleging she was not hired to be CEO of the Urban League of Flint Michigan (ULF) because ULF's board of directors' chairperson, Valaria Conorly-Moon, "did not believe [Kendall] was 'black enough' for the job."[104] The Urban League was founded in 1910 as a civil rights organization dedicated to economic empowerment to elevate the standard of living in black and historically underserved urban communities. During a meeting between Kendall and Moon, Moon made several remarks suggesting she did not think a biracial person was fit to be CEO.[105] Moon repeatedly asked Kendall why she considered herself black.[106] Moon also asked whether Kendall could identify with blacks because Moon felt it was important that the CEO identify with black people.[107]

After conducting a vote, ULF's board of directors offered the CEO position to Lorna Latham, an African American.[108] Six board members had voted for Kendall; eight had voted for Latham.[109] Moon voted for Latham.[110] However, even assuming Moon's vote was racially discriminatory, Kendall still had to prove that Moon influenced the board's hiring decision for her failure-to-hire claim to succeed.[111] The court explained,

> In order for Moon's comments to be imputed to the board, plaintiff [the complainant] must show that Moon, and whichever board member(s) she may have influenced, provided the "deciding margin" in selecting Latham. Since plaintiff lost by a vote of six to eight, plaintiff must show that Moon influenced at least one board member to vote for Latham, as the "deciding margin" in this case was two votes—Moon's and one other.[112]

Kendall did not provide evidence that Moon influenced the votes of any of the other seven of fourteen board members who had not voted for her.[113] Without evidence that the presumably biased decision maker influenced the necessary votes against the complainant, the court had no choice but to dismiss the case.[114] Thus, as the previous cases illustrate, courts have not misapprehended the nature of multiracial claims and in fact have appropriately administered them inasmuch as they have evenhandedly applied the same established laws and legal principles. Judges have not exempted multiracial claimants out of traditional antidiscrimination law. The only exception is where an employee has contracted with his employer to submit all workplace disputes to the out-of-court system of arbitration.[115]

Interestingly, the clarity of courts with regards to multiracial claims stands in stark contrast to their confusion with respect to race and color claims brought by black ethnics against employers with African American supervisors. Specifically, legal scholar Taunya Lovell Banks has traced the extent to which courts treat race and color claims brought by black ethnics like Afro descendants from Africa and the Caribbean as being preempted by the nondiscriminatory treatment of African American coworkers.[116] Her analysis demonstrates how courts treat black ethnics as being in the same black racial category as African Americans, and are thus blind to the color discrimination claims that can arise between the groups because the courts assume the racial commonality erases any bias with regard to skin color. In turn, courts presume that an employer replacing a black ethnic with an African American is immune to charges of discrimination, as is an employer who refrains from making racial slurs against African American employees while doing so against a black ethnic employee. For claimants not raising multiracial status, sharing African ancestry is judicially viewed as eliminating any other race and color cleavages.

In contrast, when multiracial complainants raise discrimination claims, courts have been amenable to treating them as distinctive from "African Americans" or presumably "unmixed" blacks. The preexisting treatment of multiracial claimants as a separate group from "unmixed" blacks and others is exactly what several multiracial-identity scholars suggest is missing from our case law. This is especially evident in the limited number of cases in which multiracial complainants present allegations more firmly rooted in anti-mixture bias, as discussed below.

Multiracial Discrimination as Genuine Mixed-Race Discrimination

As previously noted, few existing employment discrimination claims present allegations actually connected to anti-multiracial bias. Yet when they have been presented, courts have not been confused about how to properly administer the claims.[117] For example, in the 2010 case of *Nash v. Palm Beach County School District*,[118] Che Nash, a multiracial black and white complainant, brought a hostile work environment claim and racial discrimination claim that were both properly administered by the court in ways described below.[119] Nash was a physical education teacher at Olympic Heights Community High School (OHCHS) in Boca Raton, Florida, after having been unilaterally transferred there in 2004 from Boca Raton Middle School, where he taught sixth-grade science. Nash alleged that Peter Licata, the school principal (an administrator who had transferred him from the Boca Raton Middle School) made a discriminatory comment to Nash during a 2005 staff Thanksgiving luncheon.[120] Licata, while cutting the turkey, asked Nash if he wanted "white or dark meat because I know you are a little of both."[121] In May 2007, Licata told Nash that he was going to be "excessed" again (transferred to another school because of a decline in student population) for the following school year to return to Boca Raton Middle School to teach science rather than physical education, but that his salary and responsibilities would remain the same.[122] Because Nash had come to prefer teaching physical education, he instead chose to resign rather than be reassigned to another school.[123]

The court noted that the employer school did not dispute that Nash, "as an individual of mixed race, belongs to a protected class" and thus administered the claim based on that status.[124] As a result, Nash's failure to provide credible evidence that similarly situated employees who were not mixed-race were treated more favorably was viewed poorly by the court.[125] The court explicitly stated that complainant's "evidence of similarly situated non mixed-race employees . . . is nothing more than his personal opinion and conclusory allegations, which is simply insufficient to withstand summary judgment."[126] While the school principal's Thanksgiving luncheon insulting remark regarding Nash's mixed-race status certainly suggested anti-multiracial bias, the court concluded that one remark did not meet the legal standard of demonstrating "severe or pervasive harassment that altered the terms and conditions of his employment, and thereby created an abusive work environment."[127] Thus, Nash was unfortunately treated like all work harassment complainants in that courts view occasional "stray remarks" as insufficient to sustain a hostile work environment claim.[128] In short, Nash's discrimination claims were unsuccessful but not for reasons of judicial difficulty with multiraciality. In fact, the *Nash* court engaged in a very coherent mixed-race discrimination inquiry, finding that the evidence was simply insufficient.

Ironically, there is even a possibility that the court's strict adherence to Nash's request for a search for "multiracial" discrimination may have inadvertently undermined a fuller inquiry that could have detected a larger pattern of nonwhite discrimination in the workplace that adversely affected Nash. Specifically, Nash described several instances in which he and the few African American teachers at the school were treated poorly in contrast to the white teachers. For instance, when Nash was unilaterally transferred from teaching sixth-grade science at Boca Raton Middle School in 2004 to teach physical education and coach boys' basketball at Olympic Heights Community High School, Principal Licata overlooked him for two vacant sixth-grade science positions that instead were given to two new white males without Nash's seniority.

The following year, only Nash and the other basketball coaches, who were African American, were forced to give up practice facilities during the 2005 season. In 2006, when Nash requested money to purchase training equipment for the boys' basketball team, Principal Licata denied his request. By 2006, Nash was fired from his coaching position and replaced by a white male who was new to the district. Yet in March 2007, Principal Licata then proceeded to purchase ten thousand dollars' worth of weight-lifting equipment for the sole use of the football team and its white coaches. The weight room was off limits to the basketball teams and their two African American coaches.

When the context of Nash's workplace is examined from the perspective of nonwhite versus white differentiation, rather than specific multiracial animus, a stronger claim of discrimination surfaces. However, because the court was so focused on Nash's request to investigate specific multiracial animus, this broader pattern of nonwhite versus white differential treatment was overlooked. The irony here is that the court in *Nash* did exactly what multiracial-identity scholars have lobbied for—it fixed its inquiry on the specificity of Nash's personal multiracial identity. Yet the focus on personal multiracial identity lost sight of the significance of a workplace seemingly entrenched in a white over nonwhite hierarchy. The *Nash* court adhered to Nash's personal multiracial identity but did so at the expense of fully appreciating the nonwhite discrimination he likely experienced. Nevertheless, the *Nash* court utilized the parameters preferred by multiracial-identity scholars and did so with a coherent application of conventional legal doctrine.

To sum up, the existing cases display judicial clarity in the administration of multiracial claimant cases. The courts treat the claims as viable and apply antidiscrimination law in a customary manner that permits claims to succeed unless the available evidence fails to meet legal standards. The cases are not a foundation for concluding that multiracial claims are inadequately addressed. Similarly, the cases that are adjudicated not by a federal judge but by the EEOC (Equal Employment Opportunity Commission) itself because they involve federal employees also follow the pattern of treating multiracial complaints as viable claims relevant to antidiscrimination law.[129]

Why then are multiracial-identity scholars so convinced that the emerging body of multiracial-claimant cases necessitates a multiracial-specific reform of antidiscrimination law? More specifically, why are they particularly concerned with the absence of a judicial multiracial analysis of factual allegations overwhelmingly rooted in anti-black sentiment? One explanation can stem from the particular notion of discrimination as nonrecognition of personal racial identity that preoccupies many multiracial-identity scholars. These are all questions that will be explored in chapter 6. But before turning to the specifics of the personal racial identity notion of equality that multiracial-identity scholars are seemingly promoting, it will be useful to examine how multiracial claims are treated in the many discrimination contexts not otherwise analyzed in the multiracial-identity literature. Expanding the assessment beyond the employment context provides a deeper basis for evaluating the adequacy of antidiscrimination law for multiracials.

3

Multiracial Discrimination in Education

Implicit biases do not begin with black men and police. They
begin with black preschoolers and their teachers, if not earlier.
—Emma Brown, "Racial Bias among Preschool Teachers"[1]

Because the educational context was the site where the movement for
multiracial-identity recognition was launched, one might expect the
school environment to have the clearest articulation of the contours
of a multiracial-specific form of discrimination. In the 1980s, public
schools were at the center of a lobby for a multiracial-identity category
to be included on all school data forms. The movement for multiracial-
identity recognition in the public schools was the precursor to the
movement for a multiracial category on the national census form. Yet
despite the discourse about multiracial identity in public schools, the
multiracial complainants of racial discrimination in school settings, as
in all the civil rights areas discussed in this book, raise concerns about
being treated differently from white students on the basis of their nonwhite status rather than their specific mixed-race identity.[2]

Especially noteworthy is how blackness in particular is implicated
in the cases even when the multiracial claimant has not identified any
African ancestry. For instance, when sixteen-year-old Anthony Zeno,
a biracial white/Latino student arrived in 2005 for his freshman year
at Stissing Mountain High School (SMHS) in Pine Plains, New York,
his fellow students harassed him for the next three and a half years as
they repeatedly called him "nigger."[3] The court noted that Anthony was
"dark-skinned," and his mother stated that he was tormented by students "attacking his color . . . and the way he looked."[4] While it is un-
known whether Anthony's Latino ethnic origin included any African

ancestry (as Latinos can be of any race), what is clear is that those who harassed him perceived him to be of African ancestry and viewed it to be problematic.

Despite the fact that SMHS was a predominantly white institution where racial minorities represented less than 5 percent of the student population, it was located in upstate New York in a town where more Latinos and multiracial persons resided than African Americans. According to the 2000 census, closest in time to the events of 2005, the Dutchess County town of Pine Plains had 2,569 residents, of whom 1.36 percent were Latinos of any race, and 1.05 percent were from two or more races, while 0.90 percent were black, 96.26 percent were white, 0.66 percent were Native American, 0.66 percent were Asian, and 0.47 percent were from other races. In other words, Latino mixed-race identity would not have been a completely foreign concept at SMHS when Anthony arrived. Nevertheless it was Anthony's seemingly black appearance that made him vulnerable to discrimination.

Specifically, soon after Anthony's arrival as a freshman, a fellow student charged toward him screaming, "We don't want your kind here" at the same time that another student called Anthony a "nigger" and told him to go back where he came from while his attacker screamed that he would "rip [Anthony's] face off and . . . kick [his] ass."[5] The racist verbal and physical attacks were unrelenting the entire time Anthony attended the school. The attacks were so ubiquitous that there was next to no safe space for Anthony at the school. He was harassed in the cafeteria, where a student said to Anthony, "You fucking nigger. Go back to where you came from," as the student picked up a chair and started to throw it at Anthony before the student was restrained.[6] He was harassed in the bathroom, where he found graffiti on the walls warning him by his last name "Zeno is dead" and "Zeno will die."[7] He was harassed in class, where classmates repeatedly referred to him by black racialized terms like "homey," "gangster," "hood," "you're so ghetto," and "what's up my nigger."[8] He was harassed in the hallways with taunts of "nigger" on a daily basis.[9] One student not only threatened to "kick [Anthony's] black ass" but also repeatedly threatened to rape his younger sister.[10] Students taunted Anthony with references to lynching with their displays of nooses and threats to take a rope to the nearest tree. He was harassed on the school bus, where students repeatedly called him a "nigger."[11] He was harassed opening his locker. A student tampered with Anthony's locker so that when Anthony opened it, garbage spilled onto him and the metal door fell off, hitting him in the head.

Even his fellow football teammates and drama club members joined in the racial harassment. One football teammate punched Anthony as he told him that "he was going to kick [Anthony's] black ass."[12] At a football game a student again threatened to kick Anthony's "black ass" and called his sister a "slut."[13] When Anthony received a role in a drama club production of the TV show "Married with Children," a student commented that Anthony would fit the role better "if it was like a black gangster."[14] Rather than endure further harassment and try to graduate with a traditional New York State Regents diploma, Anthony chose to accept an IEP (Individualized Education Program) diploma instead. Unfortunately, students with IEP diplomas can only attend a limited number of community colleges, while four-year colleges, employers, the military, apprenticeship programs, and business or trade schools generally do not accept them.

With the arsenal of evidence regarding the racial harassment and the ill effects on his life that Anthony was able to present to the court, it is thus not surprising that the judge permitted the case to proceed to trial, where a jury granted Anthony one million dollars and the judge awarded him attorney's fees and court costs to be paid by the school district. Even as the court identified Anthony as biracial, the biracial identity did not confuse the court or adversely affect the enforcement of antidiscrimination law. Both the trial court judge and the appellate court that affirmed the trial court judgment applied Title VI of the Civil Rights Act of 1964.[15]

Title VI prohibits race and national-origin discrimination in any program that receives federal funding. Public educational institutions that receive federal funds (as most do) are subject to its mandate not to discriminate. In the educational setting, a school district is liable for intentional discrimination when it has been knowingly and "deliberately indifferent" to peer harassment of a student that has been "severe, pervasive, and objectively offensive." The court in Anthony's case found the evidence sufficient to support the jury's finding that Anthony's racial harassment was severe and that the school district failed to adequately respond to Anthony's pleas for help. In fact, when Anthony's mother complained to the school principal, he told her "this is a small town and . . . you don't want to start burning your bridges."[16]

Although the racial harassment that Anthony experienced in school as a Latino/white biracial student read as black was certainly extreme, it is unfortunately not a rare occurrence. Like Anthony, E. F. Fulton was a biracial student of African and Caucasian descent who alleged that his school district was deliberately indifferent to the racial harassment he experienced at the hands of students and teachers alike.[17] In 2011 E.F. transferred from a city school in Cincinnati, Ohio, to the Western Brown Middle School forty miles away in Mt. Orab, Ohio, where less than 1 percent of the students in the school district were African American. Shortly after his arrival, his social studies teacher, John Baird, told the students in E.F.'s class that Cincinnati was a dangerous place to live and they should take a gun when visiting because they could take a wrong turn and end up in a neighborhood that is "not white." Baird's statements were then accompanied by a PowerPoint presentation on "nice" areas of Cincinnati to visit. At the time of Baird's tirade about the dangers of nonwhites in Cincinnati, E.F. was the only student of African descent in the class and the only student who had just recently transferred from a school in Cincinnati. Rather than E.F. being welcomed to his new school, Baird's comments contributed to creating a racially hostile environment for him.

Unfortunately, Baird was not the only teacher who inappropriately verbalized his racialized opinions to E.F. and his classmates. E.F.'s American history teacher, Wendel Donathon, told the class that "the white man is the most discriminated against group in the history of the country" and attributed white men's loss of jobs to race-based affirmative action programs of inclusion. Moreover, Donathon regularly marked correct answers as incorrect on E.F.'s school work.

Like their classroom role models Donathon and Baird, the students also felt free to voice their racialized perspectives. E.F. was exposed to ongoing racial comments from students, such as "go back to the ghetto where you came from," "[black people are] never . . . as good as white people at anything," "blacks are thieves and criminals," and "blacks were only good athletes because they have extra muscles in their legs."[18] Even a basketball teammate stated, "E.F. is the reason I hate black people."[19] The chalkboard in the school athletic locker rooms had the words "No Niggers Allowed" when a visiting team from Cincinnati with a high percentage of African Americans was present.[20] When students in E.F.'s chemistry class suspected him of reporting an incident of cheating in the class, they repeatedly called him a "nigger-nark" and continued to do so even after the chemistry teachers stated that E.F. was not the informant.[21]

Despite reporting to the school officials the onslaught of racial harassment that he experienced at the school, the school district took no action to stop the harassing behavior. Thus, when the school board sought to have E.F.'s Title VI claim of racial harassment dismissed for failure to state a claim, the court denied the request. A motion to dismiss seeks to avoid a trial by dismissing cases early on that do not appear plausible on their face because they lack sufficient factual assertions. E.F.'s biracial identity did not interfere with the court's ability to ascertain that given the factual allegations, E.F. did state a viable claim of severe and pervasive harassment unremedied by a school board with a policy of deliberate indifference to the racial harassment and discrimination allegedly experienced by E.F.

Moreover, not only did the court permit the case to continue with trial preparations; the court also ordered the parties to enter into settlement discussions after it also denied the school district's motion for summary judgment dismissal of the case. Thereafter, the parties entered into a confidential settlement agreement.[22] Regardless of what the ultimate particulars were of the settlement agreement, it is clear that the court properly applied the law and accorded E.F. a full consideration of his claims of racial discrimination that permitted the case to be successfully resolved. Nor is E.F.'s ability to successfully reach a settlement agreement a rare occurrence for multiracial claimants.[23]

Courts have also acknowledged multiracial identity in racially hostile environment cases where the claimants failed to prove that the school boards did not properly respond to the concerns with harassment.[24] For instance, J.K. and D.K. were biracial siblings (of black and white ancestry) who alleged racial harassment in the Westport, Connecticut, public schools where they were sometimes the only children of color in their respective classes from 2001 to 2008.[25] The children attended the public schools from kindergarten through ninth grade in the Westport community, well known as an elite white suburban enclave within a sixty-seven-minute train commute to New York City. The children were told at various times by their classmates that "Blacks shouldn't live in Westport; they're only really good for making stuff in factories," and were called the "N word."[26] They were also teased about the texture of their hair and color of their skin.

However, on each occasion in which the schools were informed of the racial commentary, they responded with an attempt to remedy the situation. The Long Lots Elementary School responded by urging their entire staff to insert "teachable moment[s]" to "consciously infuse diversity awareness throughout the day."[27] The court also found that the school officials were responsive to the needs of the children in their repeated meetings with the parents, and that as a result the school district could not be viewed as deliberately indifferent to the racial harassment the children experienced. Title VI only provides for legal relief for school racial harassment where school districts have been "deliberately indifferent" in poorly responding to student reports of harassment.

Even when multiracial claimants are not ultimately successful in court, the education context is replete with judges who treat the multiracial identity like all other racial identities as subject to antidiscrimination law.[28] Such was the case for Brison Jackson, a thirteen-year-old biracial student (of black and white ancestry) at the T. M. McDonald Junior High School in Katy, Texas, who in 1994 alleged that he was treated differently from nonminority students in the manner in which he was disciplined for school infractions.[29] When the school district argued that Brison was not a member of a racial group protected class with the right to file a racial discrimination complaint, the judge immediately disagreed and permitted the case to proceed.

Brison only lost his case when he failed to provide objective evidence that any other students were disciplined differently for the same school infractions that Brison committed. Absent a proffer of objective evidence of differential treatment, the court was compelled to dismiss Brison's case. Brison received conduct slips for his disruptive behavior of knocking on classroom walls, throwing things in class, and arguing with other students. Inasmuch as schools are authorized to impose a code of conduct that promotes learning, the court noted that Brison's failure to provide any evidence of differential treatment "between white students and those of other races" warranted the summary judgment dismissal of his claim.[30]

K–12 is not the only context in which multiracial identity discrimination claims have been brought. Sean Smith was a student with Utah Valley University when he received low grades that he believed were discriminatory.[31] Despite the fact that from 2012 to 2013 Sean was an online student who never facially interacted with his instructors, the court still searched Sean's complaint for any allegations that the online instructors had access to his college application with his designation of a "Mixed race Native American" racial identity, or otherwise knew of his racial identity for purposes of discrimination. Sean's claim was ultimately dismissed not because of any court confusion with his multiracial identity but for his failure to assert how his instructors had an intent to discriminate against him in the grading system or whether white students were provided preferential treatment like permission to submit untimely assignments.

Nor have courts treated multiracial discrimination claims with nonchalance when the complainant's identity seemingly shifts between whiteness and biracial identity depending upon context. For example, in R.L.'s 2013 lawsuit against the Baldwin County Board of Education in Alabama, his mother identified him as "biracial."[32] In contrast, in school records R.L.'s mother identified him as solely white. R.L.'s mother also testified in the court case that her son was white and that she never thought of him as a minority student. R.L. himself testified in the case at the age of sixteen that he considered himself to be white. After noting the variation in the court record regarding R.L.'s racial identity, the court still proceeded to assess R.L.'s legal claim that as a biracial student of color he was treated differently from white students. In fact, the court gave no weight to the school principal's assertion that the school did not consider R.L. to be a minority student. Instead, the court accepted the biracial identity asserted by R.L. in the legal complaint and sought evidence of the discrimination that R.L. alleged.

R.L. alleged that minority students like himself in the fourth through sixth grades were disciplined more frequently and severely than white students. Specifically, R.L. alleged that he was placed in on-campus suspension (OCS) more frequently than white students and disciplined with the harsher form of exclusion into what he called "enclosed cubicles" but that the high school described as wooden study carrels forty-eight inches high in which students could be seen when they stood up or raised their hands. It was the school's practice to seat students at the study carrels located outside of the main office when restricted to on-campus suspension. OCS students were also placed in a small unoccupied office in the library. In addition, study carrels could be brought into a classroom for students such as R.L. who had difficulty focusing or staying in his seat when distracted by other students.

R.L. failed to present any evidence that white students were not subjected to the same treatment and punishment for similar misconduct as himself (such as throwing papers across a classroom, running around, or talking back). In fact R.L.'s mother admitted under oath that she had no knowledge of whether minority students were disciplined more frequently than nonminority students, or whether R.L. was treated differently than any other student. Absent any probative evidence of differential treatment, the court was compelled to dismiss the case. Thus, R.L. lost the lawsuit, but not as a result of any judicial resistance to his assertion of biracial identity.

In fact, courts appear receptive to the assertions of multiracial identity in discrimination cases even when the harm being raised is more accurately categorized as a concern with preserving a sense of white privilege. In order to understand case examples of how white privilege can be manifested in multiracial discrimination cases, it is important to explain what it exactly is. Feminist scholar Peggy McIntosh has famously described white privilege as "an invisible package of unearned assets which [one] can count on cashing in each day, but about which [one] was 'meant' to remain oblivious."[33] Included within that invisible package is the luxury to presume that race and racism are not typically relevant to one's daily life because whiteness is not thought to be a race.[34] Whiteness, within white privilege, is race-less and is instead the norm against which other groups are racialized. Engagement with race consciousness is viewed as completely optional. As a result, any unsolicited interaction regarding race and racism can be interpreted as an unwarranted imposition and interference with a color-blind life. It is this latter aspect that is especially articulated in some of the multiracial discrimination cases.

The desired "right to be race-less" was implied in the case of a biracial-identified mother who in 2012 was upset to be greeted in Spanish by Portland, Oregon, Rigler School officials and handed Spanish-language materials with which to enroll her children in an elementary school with a two-way dual Spanish immersion program. In her first amended complaint, Jasmine Dove-Anna Jones described herself as "light-skinned with a unique and attractive mix of ambiguous physical features, none of which reveal any evidence of her African-American ancestry [and stated that she] possesses a multiracial ancestry and appearance and is regularly mistaken to have one or another of a wide variety of racial and national origins; for example Chinese, Japanese, Hispanic and Hawaiian."[35] After Jasmine informed the school officials that she spoke English and was not of Hispanic origin, they proceeded to provide her with the correct English-language enrollment forms. Because the school serves over five hundred students from a variety of cultural backgrounds, it provides materials in Chinese, Russian, Somali, and Vietnamese in addition to Spanish and English. It was not Jasmine's contention that any racially different treatment resulted after she corrected the school about its blunder. Hence, the court dismissed Jasmine's racial discrimination claim because she produced no support for the contention that being mistaken for another race or ethnicity and being greeted in a foreign language based on that mistake is itself an act of discrimination. Nor did she provide evidence as to how she was harmed by that mistake.

Given the fact that Jasmine described herself as being frequently mistaken for other races (but never black), it seems incongruous that she would perceive the school's mistake as so egregious. What then could have motivated Jasmine to file a legal claim based on the incident (albeit included in a larger lawsuit about the mistreatment of her learning disabled son)? Being presumed to be of a particular race immediately reveals that another person views you as having a race. Hence, being greeted in Spanish and handed Spanish-language school enrollment forms disrupted Jasmine's ability to conduct herself as being so racially ambiguous that she was race-less. As Jasmine emphasized that her African ancestry was not at all apparent in her appearance, it would seem that what she was seeking was to have her more apparent white ancestry be accompanied by the white privilege of not being viewed as having a race.

However, antidiscrimination law only prohibits actions that cause tangible adverse harm. The law does not issue sanctions for speculating about another's racial identity, presuming it is a nonwhite identity, and then being mistaken in what is guessed. Absent some proffer from Jasmine as to how the reaction to her racial ambiguity harmed her, she presented the court with an incoherent claim of discrimination. However, it would be inaccurate to attribute the incoherence to the fact that Jasmine was not represented by a lawyer.

Indeed, incoherent claims of multiracial discrimination resounding in desires for white privilege can exist in even the most high-profile of cases led by expert lawyers. One of the most well known of multiracial education-discrimination cases that garnered much media attention was filed in 1997, by Bethany Godby, a thirteen-year-old biracial student of white and black ancestry who was barred from running to be the white homecoming queen of the Cloverdale Junior High in Montgomery, Alabama.[36] The school had a practice of electing two separate homecoming queens, one white and one black. The racially segregated election system originated in the 1960s to help "smooth the transition" with school integration.[37] The practice had been discontinued by 1994 but was reinstituted after complaints from white students and their parents dismayed by the greater frequency with which black homecoming queens were elected as the school became more racially integrated. During the 1995–1996 school year, the school reported itself as 91 percent black and 9 percent nonblack.[38]

School officials informed Bethany in 1996 that she had to choose to compete in either the white or the black election but not both. After Bethany solicited the opinions of her classmates, the majority told her that she should run as a white nominee. But when Bethany's class selected her as their white class nominee, her name did not appear on the ballot for the schoolwide election that the school officials issued.

What is curious is that Bethany's legal complaint filed by her lawyers does not articulate a clear challenge to the white racial entitlement and racism of maintaining a racially segregated election. In fact, the court noted, "Plaintiffs [complainants] appear to be a bit unsure, as are some of the school officials, of what the particular wrong is. Is the wrong the election that was 'stolen' from Godby? Or is the wrong that there was not a separate 'biracial' category?"[39]

In her written legal complaint she asserted,

> Plaintiff [complainant] was not allowed to compete for a position on the homecoming court as a nominated "white" candidate because of Defendants' policy and practice that "two or three drops of black blood establishes that you are black"—in the words of Defendant [school principal] Wilson. Plaintiffs [complainants] seek damages for the harm caused by the Defendants' racially discriminatory customs, practices and policies at Cloverdale Junior High School.[40]

The complaint goes on to specify that the discriminatory "pattern or practice" alleged is that of "excluding, segregating, and discriminating against biracial and/or multiracial students on the basis of race," specifically because "biracial and multiracial students are not given equal opportunities at Cloverdale Junior High School."[41]

Bethany's own legal statement of her claim thus provides little critique of how inherently racist it was for all students to attend a public school that deployed a separate but equal system of dual homecoming elections. This was mirrored by media accounts that saw the problem as embedded in forcing Bethany as a biracial student to choose between white and black, rather than the structural racism all students were exposed to of having dual elections.[42]

> Children in Bethany's racial category will and should continue to speak out against a government racial classification system that compels them to deny their heritage. These children want their government to assign them a racial category that represents their individual reality. Children

born of both black and white parents want to be classified in that manner. And for Bethany Godby . . . a Biracial category will be just fine.[43]

Did Bethany simply want her name placed back on the white nominees list without having the racially segregated system dismantled? That would certainly have been a clear indication of a pursuit of white privilege through the vehicle of a multiracial discrimination claim. However, Bethany decided to settle her claim with the Montgomery County Board of Education before further clarifying her objectives for a jury trial. Racially segregated homecoming court elections continued in various Alabama school districts until as late as 2012, when the U.S. Justice Department sued to end the practice.[44]

But whether Bethany or any other multiracial claimant was ultimately pursuing white privilege or instead distressed with being discriminated against as nonwhite, both concerns highlight the continued relevance of a white/nonwhite racial binary of discrimination. In short, the educational context, like the other civil rights areas examined in this book, is one where complainants may personally identify with the fluidity of a mixed-race category, but proceed to detail instances of experiencing strictly white/nonwhite segregation and discrimination. None of the cases are incomprehensible to judges as they apply traditional antidiscrimination legal doctrines.

The salience of the white/nonwhite binary in the cases is underscored by the racial isolation that many of the multiracial students experienced in predominantly white settings described throughout this chapter.[45] It is thus apt to close this chapter with a case that illuminates the role of racial isolation in the multiracial experience of white versus nonwhite discrimination. It is the story of one father's quest to have his biracial daughter not be subjected to race-based stress from her racially exclusive high school in Wisconsin.

Brian Shelton identified himself as the African American father of a biracial daughter conceived with his former white spouse, and in 2009 he filed a lawsuit seeking to prevent his daughter from being the lone student of color in a sociology class addressing explosive racial issues.[46] Initially Brian alerted the school that he wished to have his daughter Margaret exempt from a specific class exercise in the sociology course that might subject her to particular strain as one of the few students of African descent in the school. The class assignment was entitled "A Class Divided" and asked students to write a response defending or refuting one of the following proffered statements:

1. Why is it so bad to use the word "nigger"? I hear blacks use it to each other all the time.
2. The most important things minority groups need are education and the vote.
3. I should not be held responsible for the behavior of my ancestors.
4. If you could just get people to feel good about themselves, there would be less racism.
5. The Irish and the Italians made it in this country in spite of discrimination. Why can't blacks pull themselves up by their own bootstraps, too?

As her father, Brian especially objected to the use of the word "nigger" and the focus of the assignment solely on a racial slur for African Americans rather than the many other racial slurs that exist for other minority groups, because Margaret would not have a concrete mass of other Afro-descended students or an Afro-descended instructor in the class to handle the strain of navigating the possible incendiary comments that could be raised by the classroom discussion. Thus, what Brian opposed was the enhanced potential for harm that his daughter might experience by being the only nonwhite student in a classroom during discussions of heated racial issues. His complaint was centered on Margaret's racial isolation as a nonwhite student and not any unique harms she would experience as mixed-race. When the school refused to permit Margaret to opt out of the "Class Divided" unit, her father Brian proceeded to file his lawsuit seeking her removal from the class itself.

Because Margaret's mother had sole parental custody, the court prevented Brian from moving forward with his claim. The case was thus dismissed for Brian's lack of standing to file a custodial parent–based claim. The court also noted that Brian had failed to identify how the school had a specific intent to discriminate. Like individual claims of employment discrimination under Title VII, individual claims of discrimination under Title VI in the education context also require proof of the intent to discriminate. Brian's case thus highlights the book's overarching theme regarding the continued salience of the white/nonwhite binary in multiracial discrimination cases in addition to the ways in which multiracial claimants are subject to the same challenging doctrinal demands as claimants who are not multiracial.

4

Multiracial Housing and Public Accommodations Discrimination

The real estate market today reflects an ugly, if often forgotten,
truth: Residential segregation in the U.S. is alive and well.
—Ilyce Glink, "U.S. Housing Market Remains
Deeply Segregated"[1]

"Public accommodations" are facilities that are used by the public and thus regulated by antidiscrimination law to ensure equal access by all. Examples include hotels, service centers, and recreational facilities. Housing is a form of public accommodation that is so fundamental that it has its own specific civil rights laws and enforcement structure. Given the significance of the right to fair housing, this chapter shall first address the particulars of housing discrimination before turning to public accommodations more broadly.

Housing Discrimination

Distinctive from the context of workplace discrimination, where multiracial adult complainants articulate their own legal complaints, the housing context is characterized by a dearth of such direct complaints. The issue of multiraciality in housing discrimination is instead chiefly raised by parents of multiracial children in ways that parallel the education discrimination context. The primary law for alleging housing discrimination is the Fair Housing Act (FHA) of 1968, which is commonly referred to as the "last plank of the Civil Rights Movement."[2] Congress passed the FHA in response to the race riots of the 1960s that many attributed in part to the poor living conditions wrought by residential segregation and the racialization of poverty. However, by the time the government attempted to step in, it might be said that the die had already been cast. The government had to counter decades of its previous active involvement and complicity in maintaining segregated neighborhoods, decades that had resulted in highly segregated neighborhoods.[3]

Nevertheless, the FHA's purpose was to further "the goal of open, integrated residential housing patterns and to prevent the increase of segregation."[4] In order to accomplish this, Sections 3604 and 3605 of the act make it unlawful to discriminate against a person in a residential real estate transaction on the basis of that person's inclusion in a protected class.[5] The act provides three ways of enforcing its provisions: administrative enforcement by the U.S. Department of Housing and Urban Development, federal litigation, and private litigation.[6] Furthermore, courts have expanded causes of action under FHA for some of the most common examples of indirect discrimination that contribute to residential segregation. These include "mortgage redlining, insurance redlining, racial steering, exclusionary zoning decisions, and other actions by individuals or government units which directly affect the availability of housing to minorities."[7] Within the realm of evolving multiracial claimant housing cases, the claims thus far have arisen in the context of individual claims of intentional discrimination against families that have already succeeded in obtaining housing but allege discrimination in the terms, conditions, services, or facilities in the rental of property.

The only case describing actual anti-mixture bias was an extreme scenario in which a white supremacist organization targeted a white female fair housing specialist employee and her biracial daughter for harassment from 1998 to 2000.[8] In 1998 Bonnie Jouhari worked for the Reading-Berks Human Relations Council, a private nonprofit fair-housing organization located in Reading, Pennsylvania. Bonnie was well known in the Reading civil rights community as an energetic advocate. Unfortunately, Bonnie's public recognition as an activist committed to racially integrated housing made her a target for an extremist hate group known as ALPHA HQ, whose stated purpose was to further the goals of the white supremacist movement.

ALPHA HQ posted a photo of Bonnie with a flyer of a hooded Ku Klux Klansman with a caption that read "Race Traitor Beware."[9] Below Bonnie's photograph the following information was provided: "This 'woman' works at the Reading-Berks Human Relations Council and has received warnings in the mail that she is a race traitor and she should beware. Traitors like this should beware, for in our day, they will be hung from the neck from the nearest tree or lamp post."[10] Immediately above Bonnie's photograph, the website showed an animated photographic image of her workplace, the Reading-Berks Human Relations Council, exploding into flames. Next to that image was the statement "The Reading-Berks Human Relations Council. This is the office where plans for additional race-mixing and 'integration' are planned."[11] The website page was later modified to provide a description of Bonnie's sixteen-year-old black/white biracial daughter Pilar as a "mongrel," along with a recipe for a bomb.[12]

With the incitement from the website, Bonnie and her daughter Pilar were targeted with an unrelenting campaign of harassing phone calls to their home in which funeral dirge music was played. A well-known Ku Klux Klansman made it a habit to sit outside Bonnie's office in a menacing manner and called to say that the Klan was watching her. Despite Bonnie changing their home phone number numerous times, paying to have the phone number and that of her daughter be unlisted, and reporting the incidents to the law enforcement authorities, the harassment continued. The harassment continued even after Bonnie and her daughter fled Reading, Pennsylvania, in fear to resettle across the country in Silverdale in Washington State.

The racial harassment forced Bonnie out of both her home and her job as a fair housing specialist where she could assist others to pursue fair housing. The Fair Housing Act prohibits both of those results. When Bonnie and her daughter were forced to flee the harassment once again and take an apartment in Kent, Washington, with their telephone service listed in the name of a friend, the harassing phone calls still continued. Bonnie then filed a claim for Fair Housing Act racial discrimination before the U.S. Department of Housing and Urban Development (HUD— the agency responsible for enforcing the Fair Housing Act) for the racial harassment that interfered with her and her daughter's ability to live in their home, and with her work of assisting others with their Fair Housing Act concerns.

Thus in the one case in which concrete anti-mixture animus is expressed with the use of the epithet "mongrel," it is part of a Jim Crow–era form of white supremacist harassment, rather than evidencing a new form of racism with the rise of multiracial identity. In response to the claim, the administrative law judge (ALJ) ordered ALPHA HQ to pay Bonnie $283,683.64 in damages, and pay Pilar $827,793.75 in damages for the disruption and emotional damage to their lives. In addition to being enjoined from further harassing Bonnie and Pilar, a $55,000 civil penalty was also imposed for payment to HUD as part of the Fair Housing Act's deterrence efforts. The extant antidiscrimination law operated effectively to redress the biracial discrimination that was embedded in ALPHA HQ's animus against all nonwhites. The ALJ recognized the white supremacist discrimination Pilar experienced from being targeted as a "mongrel" and authorized that she obtain full compensation. It is therefore difficult to conceive of any multiracial-recognition law reform that could have better addressed Pilar's injuries.

Apart from the exceptional circumstances of the ALPHA HQ white supremacist animus against a biracial teenager, the vast majority of housing discrimination cases fail to evidence any specific anti-mixture sentiment.[13] Moreover, only one case has ever been filed by a multiracial-identified adult as opposed to the parents of multiracial children. The one singular multiracial adult–initiated complaint of housing discrimination occurred in 2008.[14]

At that time, Meki Bracken, a woman of African American and Samoan background, sought to sublet a room in Chicago. But when Meki came to view the premises, the landlord indicated that he did not wish to consider a "black applicant." The landlord subsequently advertised the room as available and rented it to someone else of another race.

Meki filed a complaint with HUD. After HUD investigated the complaint, HUD decided there was reasonable cause to believe discrimination occurred. Meki then elected to have her claim heard before a HUD ALJ. The benefit of choosing to proceed with a claim before an ALJ rather than filing the claim in a federal court is that ALJ administrative proceedings are thought to be more streamlined and processed more quickly than court proceedings.

When the landlord failed to respond to the ALJ proceedings, a default decision was entered and Meki was awarded $49,284.00 in damages. An award of damages in housing cases can include compensation for tangible economic losses, emotional distress, and inconvenience.[15] While the ALJ did refer to Meki as a "racial minority" who "is African-American" rather than fully acknowledge her multiracial identity, he nevertheless meticulously processed her claim and understood the harm of the discrimination that specifically targeted her African ancestry. As a result, Meki was able to successfully resolve her legal case of discrimination.

In contrast to the Meki Bracken case, the vast majority of multiracial housing claims are brought not by multiracial adult complainants themselves, but instead by the white relatives of multiracial children.[16] Remarkably, each electronically available case studied in this chapter resulted in a favorable judgment for the claimant (except for one administratively time-barred claim).[17] As has been previously noted, winning judgments are the rarity for most other discrimination complainants of color.

One paradigmatically successful multiracial housing discrimination case is of a white mother's challenge to a 2003 eviction in Ohio based upon the landlord's expressed prejudice against her two biracial sons of white and black ancestry.[18] In October 2003, Donna Cousins sought to rent a single-family home in South Salem, Ohio, a town with a population size of approximately 213 people, of which 96.24 percent were white, .94 percent were black, .47 percent were Native American, and

.94 percent were from other races. In addition, 1.41 percent identified with two or more races, and Latinos of any race were 1.41 percent of the population. Donna and her partner, Rick James, were looking for a rental property after their home was foreclosed and they were forced to declare bankruptcy. In dire straits, they sought to rent a house that was located directly in front of the landlord's logging business.

When Donna and Rick were shown the rental home, they informed the landlord that Donna had two sons who were not then present. Donna did not inform the landlord that her sons were biracial. Donna, Rick, and the landlord and his wife were all white. Donna and her family moved into the rental home in August 2003 and lived there without incident until October 22, 2003. On October 22, 2003, the landlord's wife came by Donna's home to collect payment for a fuel bill and entered the living room and saw photos of Donna's sons. The very next day the landlord's wife delivered a three-day notice to vacate the premises.

There was very little doubt regarding the race-based motivation behind the eviction notice. During a telephone conversation with Rick's sister, the landlord's wife said that she "didn't realize they had two black boys" and that she wanted the "thieving niggers" out of the house. Similarly, the landlord himself referred to Donna's sons as "niggers, Afros and hucklebucks" that he wanted out of the house. When Donna and Rick attempted to pay the November 2003 rent by placing a money order in the landlord's mailbox, the landlord came to their home to return the money with the statement, "I don't want your money; I want your . . . niggers out of my house."

While the landlord and his wife denied all these allegations, the court in its review of all the evidence remarked that Donna and Rick and all their witnesses were more credible than the landlord and his witnesses. The court found it particularly notable that neither the three-day notice to vacate the premises nor the notice to terminate the vacancy provided any specific reasons for commencing the eviction proceeding. In fact, conventional equality law equates the absence of any proffer of a non-discriminatory rationale in combination with the presentation of some discriminatory animus as adequate proof of discrimination. For this reason, the court found that Donna and Rick were entitled to the preliminary injunction they sought preventing the landlord from evicting them in violation of the Fair Housing Act prohibition against denying housing to any person on account of race.[19]

In according Donna and Rick their legal victory and later awarding them attorney's fees when the landlord violated the preliminary injunction by harassing them,[20] the court consistently referenced the discrimination as being based on the presence of two "biracial sons." Thus this was a court that respected the complainant's personal identity in exactly the way that multiracial-identity scholars are lobbying for. Yet it should be noted that while Donna described her sons' personal racial identities as biracial, the discrimination she delineated was rooted in societal anti-black bias. Thus, the very evidence that the court relied upon to determine that racial discrimination had occurred all emanated from the derogatory statements made not about being racially mixed but rather about the African ancestry portion of the mixture.

Proving housing discrimination is often eased by the additional research that a nonprofit organization can provide.[21] Michele Jones benefited from such assistance. Michele Jones was a white mother who encountered discrimination in 2002, based on her association with African Americans and the black-white biracial status of her daughter Mikayla in the white-dominated town of Saraland, Alabama, a suburb of Mobile, Alabama. In the 2000 census, whites represented 88.5 percent of Saraland's population, while blacks represented 8.97 percent, and only 1.13 percent of the population selected two or more races. Michele rented a unit at "Bea's Trailer Park" after a friend who was an existing tenant of the park communicated Michele's interest to the owner.[22]

After Michele moved in and a black friend and coworker came to visit her, the owner stated, "I saw a nigger at your house earlier. I don't want any trouble with the neighbors."[23] The owner later asked a tenant whether she knew whether Michele dated black men or invited black people to her parties or to spend the night. When the tenant responded that Michele had black friends and a black-white biracial daughter, the owner said that she did not want any blacks in the house and that "they know they are not supposed to be in the park after 5:00 p.m."[24] In fact, no other black tenants lived on the property at that time or any time in the previous seven years.

The owner then proceeded to pay Michele a visit and inform her that "[e]veryone around here knows that I don't let those people come around here. If I had known that you were like that, with a mixed child, you would have never come here. . . . I don't care what the government says about this. I don't want to see any more Black people at your house."[25] Despite the fact that according to Michele, her eighteen-month-old daughter Mikayla's "ethnicity was not apparent," the owner further stated that the next time she rented to anyone, she would "make sure she looked the kids in the face real good."[26] Approximately two days later, the owner told Michele that she needed to find somewhere else to live.

After moving out because the owner continued to harass her about having black guests, Michele contacted the Mobile Fair Housing Center, a nonprofit fair housing advocacy organization, and they conducted two fair housing tests of the property. The fair housing test consisted of sending in an interracial couple with a biracial minor daughter to seek housing at the property, and later a white family to do the same. Evidence of housing discrimination is often ferreted out through such paired studies. When the multiracial tester family sought out housing at the property, the owner informed them that nothing was available. When the white family sought out housing that same day, the owner indicated that there were several lots available and showed them to the white tester family.

Given the extent of evidence against the owner, it is not surprising that she agreed to settle the case.[27] The owner agreed to compensate Michele and her daughter $19,000, to pay Michele's attorney $8,000, to pay the Mobile Fair Housing Center $10,000, and to pay a $5,000 civil penalty to the U.S. government. Furthermore, the consent order also mandated that the owner was enjoined from discriminating, and was required to prepare, implement, post, and disseminate a nondiscriminatory policy, to undergo certified fair housing training along with all other employees involved in renting or managing any of the units, to keep detailed records about the application and rental of all units, including the race of the applicants, and to report on all compliance efforts to the U.S. government every six months for three years or longer should the consent order be extended.

Besides the comprehensive victory for Michele and Mikayla, what is notable about the case is the manner in which the owner's references to Mikayla's mixed status as objectionable were all directly linked to her African ancestry and the owner's animus against all blacks. While the owner may have made pejorative statements about race mixture, the context of her remarks indicates a fundamental anti-black hostility regardless of mixture.

Unfortunately, the particularized anti-black experience of multiracial exclusion does not seem to be altered by its occurrence in a much larger and more diverse city like Chicago, Illinois, whose population in 1990 alone was 7.4 million. Such was the case for the Horwick family.[28] When the Horwick family was subject to a racially motivated eviction in the 1990s, their city of Chicago was 66.10 percent white, 19.01 percent black, 11.36 percent Latino, and 3.45 percent Asian. Despite the racial diversity of their city, they discovered that the apartment building in which they resided was a white racial enclave. In fact, while Charles Horwick is white, his wife Barbara Horwick was one of only two black tenants living in the building. When a new owner and management company took over the apartment building in December 1990, seven days thereafter the company served eviction notices only on the Horwicks, their two biracial daughters, and the only other black tenant, while at the same time renewing the leases of the white tenants.

In addition to the eviction notices, the landlord used a harassment campaign of repeated visits and phone calls to urge the black tenants to move out. Moreover, the landlord directly harassed the Horwick multiracial daughters Sarah and Alia, ages twelve and eighteen. The apartment building manager questioned the Horwick daughters as to whether they lived in the apartment and what they were doing there. When they informed the manager that they lived there and had their own key, the manager responded that he had better change the lock. He then followed the girls to school.

While the manager never made any disparaging comments about the Horwick girls' mixed-race ancestry, he was fixated on what he perceived to be their nonwhiteness. Taken in the context of the overarching anti-black targeting of the landlord, it would appear that the Horwick girls' black ancestry was most salient to the racial animus they experienced. Indeed, the court specifically noted, "There is no dispute that plaintiffs [complainants, including the daughters] belong to a minority and that defendants knew that."[29] The court then permitted the case to proceed to a jury trial. Thereafter, the parties decided to file a settlement agreement with the court. In short, the court treated the allegations of discrimination as legitimate and then proceeded to appropriately enforce the law with a jury trial. It is difficult to discern any deficiency with the content or application of law caused by having a multiracial claimant.

Like the Horwick family, the George and Theresia White family are an interracial family who in 1994 were excluded from a desired housing unit because of the landlord's hostility towards the African ancestry of its multiracial members.[30] What is noteworthy about the case is the manner in which the court alludes to the impact of exclusionary white spaces on multiracial children. The White family lived in Chicago but wished to move to an apartment in the nearby suburb of Hickory Hills, Illinois, near Theresia's workplace. Theresia (who is white) saw a "For Rent" sign in front of the landlord's twelve-unit Hickory Hills apartment building and called to make an inquiry. The landlord indicated that there was an apartment available, and they made an appointment for Theresia to view the apartment. When Theresia arrived for the appointment with her husband George (who is a person of African and American Indian ancestry who racially identifies himself as black), they were told that the unit had already been rented. However, when Theresia telephoned the landlord one hour later, he indicated that the apartment actually was still available. He then asked whether she was black or white because he said he did not want blacks in the building. The apartment remained vacant for over two months until the landlord rented it to a white person.

As a result, the ALJ ordered the landlord to pay the White family $93,000 in damages in addition to a civil penalty to HUD of $11,000. The ALJ order also directed the landlord to institute specific race-conscious record keeping about its applicants and tenants and to report the data on a monthly basis to HUD for the following three years for monitoring. The White family not only won their case, but they also obtained a full recognition of and compensation for the harm they experienced.

While the landlord never met the Whites' three mixed-race children, the ALJ took special note of the harms that the children endured because of the landlord's discriminatory action as it was the children's first encounter with racism of any kind. Prior to the search for an apartment in Hickory Hills, the White family lived in the predominantly black neighborhood of Engelwood, Chicago. While living there, neither Theresia, George, nor their mixed-race children "suffered any racial discrimination problems."[31] Nor did they experience racial discrimination when they previously lived in a neighborhood of "mostly working class black people" in Buffalo, New York.[32] Only when the White family attempted to move into the "mostly white neighborhood" of the Hickory Hills, Chicago suburb did the children feel the sting of discrimination.[33] Their mixed-race ancestry as the children of a white parent and a parent of African and Native American ancestry only became a source of hostility when their African ancestry was not welcomed into an exclusionary white space.

Even in jurisdictions where nonwhites numerically outnumber whites, the housing discrimination multiracial claimants describe pertains to the negative reactions to nonwhiteness rather than racial mixture per se.[34] For instance in 2010, when Angela Alexander, a white mother of biracial children, sought to rent a mobile home in Pine Bluff, Arkansas, she encountered great hostility to the black ancestry of her children.[35] While Pine Bluff, Arkansas, is a town where in 2010, approximately 75.5 percent of the population described themselves as black, 21.8 percent as white, and 1.1 percent as more than one race, the landlord of the mobile home informed Angela that she had never rented to blacks and was not going to begin doing so with her children because all the neighbors were white.[36] Moreover, the landlord indicated that her husband would refuse to make home repairs for Angela and her children and that it would be better for everyone to deny Angela the mobile home. After rejecting Angela and her children as tenants, the landlord proceeded to rent the mobile home to a white family.

Angela filed a claim with HUD and the parties settled the case. By virtue of the settlement agreement, the landlord was required to pay Angela $1,250 in damages. In addition, the landlord was obligated to submit to HUD supervision for a two-year period during which HUD would be allowed to inspect all tenant and application records for evidence of further exclusion. For Angela and her multiracial children, antidiscrimination law was fully enforced to vindicate their claims.

The only reported housing cases in which a multiracial racial discrimination claim did not succeed was one where the claimant failed to offer any evidence of the alleged discrimination.[37] The other was a case where the court administratively was barred from considering the substantive claims. This occurred because the complaint was not filed by the statute of limitations deadline, and the claimants signed an order agreeing to evictions for nonpayment of rent.[38]

In short, as in the employment context discussed in chapter 2, and the education context discussed in chapter 3, the content of the housing discrimination complaints are focused on the hostility with nonwhiteness and blackness in particular, as opposed to the particularities of a distinctive anti-mixture animus. This is a consistent pattern regardless of geographic location or demographic differences across the country. The stories of nonwhite animus against multiracial victims looks the same. None of the claims raise a concern with multiracial-focused forms of segregation. Nor do they raise a multiracial-specific concern with what has historically been the fundamental aim of the Fair Housing Act—dismantling residential racial segregation. In other words, the reported multiracial housing claims do not suggest multiracial-specific ghettoes are being constructed with their exclusion from white spaces. In stark contrast to the multiracial-identity scholars' concern with the unique position of multiracial discrimination, the housing context illuminates the great extent to which multiracial claimants experience historic white versus nonwhite forms of discrimination that courts have traditionally addressed.

In fact, there are even times when the housing discrimination reaches the level of a traditional Jim Crow crime because of the use of violence and intimidation. This occurred in 2006, when Nathaniel Reed (a biracial man with black ancestry) had his mobile home in Independence, Missouri, vandalized and defaced with the red and black ink writing of "nigger," "porch monkey," "fucking jungle bunnie [sic]," "KKK is looking for you," "KKK is going to find you," "lets [sic] go coon hunting," and "white power," along with other racially derogatory slurs and the drawing of swastikas.[39] The assailants then set Nathaniel's home on fire with the intention of forcing him to move away. Each aspect of the case had the hallmarks of a white supremacist conspiracy except for one. Here the United States Department of Justice actually prosecuted the assailants for the federal crime of conspiring and using threats and intimidation to interfere with the constitutional right to occupy real property without injury.[40]

The assailants then pled guilty, were incarcerated for forty-two months followed by three years of supervised release, and ordered to pay $35,509 of restitution to Nathaniel. Racial progress can certainly be located in the fact that Nathaniel's attackers were prosecuted and he received some restitution. Yet Nathaniel's biracial identity did not mitigate in any way his exposure to white supremacist violence. All that mattered to the assailants was that Nathaniel was nonwhite. The public accommodation context examined in the next section reveals a similar pattern of multiracial discrimination rooted in bias against nonwhites.

Public Accommodations Discrimination

Unlike all the other civil rights topics discussed in this book, the public accommodations context stands out as the one basis of discrimination in which the presence of multiracial complainants is very limited in number. Several factors may account for why there are so few multiracial cases in the public accommodations context as opposed to other discrimination areas. In contrast to many other discrimination contexts, like those of housing, education, and employment, where multiracial cases are more numerous, in accessing public accommodations neither the complainant nor his or her personal racial identity is likely to be known by the perpetrator of discrimination. Rather, the biased exclusion is based solely upon physical perception in ways that diminish the salience of personal identity.

The absence of the assertion of multiracial identity in public accommodations litigation—the quintessential context for traditional, Jim Crow, stark-black-white-binary discrimination—underscores the extent to which multiracials are targeted for discrimination on the basis not of their mixed-race status but rather of their physical appearance as racialized subjects or knowledge about their nonwhite racial ancestry. The language of the original public accommodation statute is explicit in its concern with addressing white supremacy.

The original statutory prohibition against discrimination in public accommodations was enacted as part of the Civil Rights Act of 1866. The act was passed to further the U.S. Constitution's 1865 Thirteenth Amendment abolition of slavery by ensuring that newly freed slaves would not be effectively reenslaved by the exclusion of nonwhites from full engagement in civic society and commerce. The pertinent statutory language is codified in 42 U.S.C. § 1981 as "all persons . . . shall have the same right in every State and Territory to make and enforce contracts . . . as is enjoyed by *white* citizens."

The statute does not demand that complainants assert any particular "monoracial" racial identity but simply that they articulate how they were treated differently from those identified solely as white. Thus the legal claim is open to multiracial claimants along with claimants of any other racial identity. Furthermore, the Supreme Court has also interpreted the statute to prohibit discrimination against whites as well.[41]

Today the major federal statute used to challenge public accommodations discrimination is Title II of the 1964 Civil Rights Act. Title II entitles all people "[t]o the full and equal enjoyment of the goods, services, facilities, privileges, advantages, and accommodations of any place of public accommodation, as defined in this section, without discrimination or segregation on the ground of race, color, religion, or national origin" (42 U.S.C. §§ 2000a et seq.). A major advantage of Title II is that it authorizes the U.S. Department of Justice (DOJ) to bring a lawsuit when there is reason to believe that a person has engaged in a pattern or practice of public accommodations discrimination. Having the DOJ with all of its resources file a larger-scale pattern and practice claim is less burdensome on individual claimants who would otherwise have to litigate the claim on their own. In addition, the ability to identify patterns and practices of discrimination that extend beyond an individual claimant can result in greater institutional reforms.

However, the DOJ has yet to file a single pattern or practice claim related to allegations of multiracial discrimination. One could speculate that the absence of DOJ claims simply reflects a governmental oversight. But when considered in the context of the dearth of individual claims as well, the DOJ inaction might be better understood as reflecting the actual absence of uniquely multiracial claims. The content of the few individual claims filed supports the premise that a distinctive form of multiracial discrimination has not yet been articulated.

One of the few multiracial public accommodations cases available in the Westlaw electronic database of court opinions is that of Walter Jefferson.[42] Walter alleged that the municipal Fremont Tennis Center (FTC) in Fremont, California, discriminated against him in 2009 because he was a "biracial minority" and "African American" tennis captain. Walter further alleged that when the FTC appointed a new tennis director named Jeff Gonce, Gonce allowed an FTC employee to call Walter a "Black bastard," and prohibited him and other minority tennis captains from being able to reserve and use the public tennis courts for their teams while stating, "You people are always complaining."[43] Thus, while Walter personally identified as biracial, he articulated allegations rooted in a white versus nonwhite division at the FTC.

The court treated Walter's claim as viable and denied multiple attempts to have the case dismissed from 2012 through 2014. In fact, the court allowed Walter to amend his complaint three separate times and engage in discovery where various witness testimonies were taken in deposition. Only after Walter's own witnesses and teammates denied that any discrimination occurred at FTC did the court ultimately dismiss the case for failure to proffer evidence to support the allegations of discrimination.

In contrast, the FTC provided documentation that Walter's chronic failure to follow the FTC rules for making a reservation, along with his frequently tardy payments, were the reasons he encountered delays in being able to reserve a court. Furthermore, the court also found that FTC's policy change to provide priority to Fremont residents when the demand for court space was high disproportionately affected non-Fremont white tennis captains. Walter was not a Fremont resident, but three of the four tennis captains affected by the new residency rules were white. Without a statistical adverse effect on multiracials or other non-whites, or other evidence of discrimination, Walter had no support for his claim. The court thoroughly searched the record for any evidence of discrimination without imposing any particular limits related to Walter's biracial identity. In short, the judicial administration of Walter's case was not adversely affected by his biracial identity.

Even cases where the claimants proceed pro se (without legal representation) and thus risk an incomplete articulation of their legal claim, courts have shown a receptivity to multiracial claims. Damien Kilgore filed a lawsuit in 2016 challenging the behavior of a security guard at the Providence Place Mall in Providence, Rhode Island, who asked him to move and allegedly harassed him as he was waiting for a ride.[44] Damien stated that his "biracial citizenship" was what prompted the security guard to harass him on the occasion in question, and caused Providence Place Mall to harass him on a daily basis.

Despite the fact that Damien failed to provide any details as to how others who were waiting for rides were treated differently than himself or other details as to how his racial background was the cause of his treatment, the court refrained from dismissing the case for failure to state a claim. Instead the court provided Damien with an additional thirty days to file an amended complaint with the additional factual allegations the court requested. Damien did not avail himself of the opportunity to file an amended complaint, and his case was dismissed without prejudice (which permits him to refile an amended complaint in the future).[45] Consequently, there is no further information about the discrimination Damien believes he experienced. Nevertheless, what is clear from even this thin record is that the court treated Damien's pursuit to vindicate his perceived "biracial citizenship" discrimination with respect and consideration. Nor was Damien's judge singular in his respectful treatment of a multiracial public accommodations claim.

Aretha Brown also filed a pro se claim in 2014 based upon her perception of discrimination based upon her "multiracial" background.[46] When Aretha was a job applicant and guest at the Luxor Hotel in Las Vegas, Nevada, she attempted to enter the Luxor Hotel LAX Nightclub. She alleged that after purchasing her ticket, the Luxor security staff voided her ticket, removed her by force from the line, and later photographed her and banned her from the premises. Aretha asserted that the security personnel repeatedly uttered racially derogatory remarks as they harassed her.

But as in Damien's case against the Providence Place Mall, Aretha failed to detail how she was treated less favorably than individuals of other races seeking to enter the nightclub. Aretha's judge also granted her an additional thirty days to file an amended complaint with greater detail. When Aretha failed to file an amended complaint based upon the mistaken belief that filing a separate employment discrimination claim with the Equal Employment Opportunity Commission would satisfy the judge's request for greater detail, the court once again accorded her another thirty days to file an amended complaint, and yet another three-month extension thereafter. It is quite noteworthy that the trial court judge granted the additional time on three separate occasions despite the fact that the magistrate judge recommended that the trial judge dismiss the complaint with prejudice (thereby foreclosing the ability to file a more detailed complaint later in time). The trial judge noted that Aretha manifested a "fundamental misunderstanding about the judicial process that [made] dismissal inappropriate at this time."[47] A year and a half later, the trial judge allowed the case to remain open while Aretha searched for a lawyer to represent her. Aretha was thus accorded every opportunity to vindicate her belief that her multiracial background motivated a discriminatory denial of access to the Luxor Hotel LAX Nightclub. A greater example of judicial consideration and respect would be hard to find. Only when Aretha failed to comply with any of the court deadlines was her case dismissed over two years after she filed her claim.[48]

Courts continue to accord multiracial claims due consideration even when multiracial claimants articulate factual allegations in which multiracial identity seems somewhat tangential to the discrimination alleged. For instance, Angela and Johnny are parents who filed a claim against the Harrisburg Soccer Club of Harrisburg, Pennsylvania, on behalf of their ten-year-old "mixed race" daughter Johnae Robinson in 2007.[49] In the complaint, the Robinsons, who are a black and white interracial couple, specified that "Johnae is equally proud of her black and white heritage. Many of Johnae's best friends are white."[50] Their concern with discrimination arose when Erik Hicks, the Harrisburg Soccer Club (HSC) president, made a reference to race during an April 11, 2007, pregame team meeting. Hicks stated to Johnae's team, which was comprised primarily of nonwhite players, "We're going to kick those white girls' butts." Hicks was referring to members of the opposing team. While Hicks's comment did not refer to multiraciality or target Johnae in any particular way, the Robinsons were concerned that making such a comment "to a mixed race child . . . teaches her to single other students out on the basis of race [and] categorizes children on an irrational basis."[51]

The Robinsons then launched a campaign to have Hicks fired with relentless calls and e-mails to the soccer club officials. After verbal altercations with staff and verbal harassment of the players, Mrs. Robinson was banned from attendance or communication with the HSC personnel and officials. When Mrs. Robinson continued to harass the HSC personnel and officials regarding her discontent with Mr. Hicks as a "racist" and her proffer of another individual to replace him, HSC suspended Johnae for one year from playing with HSC. HSC then offered to fund Johnae's registration fee with a neighboring soccer club "so that her soccer development would not be hampered."[52] HSC emphasized that their decision to suspend Johnae was based solely upon the behavior of her parents and their discontent with the soccer club.

The Robinsons filed an appeal of Johnae's one-year suspension, but when their behavior became threatening and aggressive, they were asked to leave and Johnae's suspension was increased from one to two years on the basis of a litany of abusive behavior from the Robinsons. The minutes of the HSC suspension appeal hearing referenced the following incidents that all preceded Johnae's August 2007 suspension from HSC:

September 06—Mrs. Robinson called club registrar/coordinator (Patricia Flores) and told her she had an older daughter that would take care of anyone on the team who wanted to start fights with her daughter.
September 06—Mrs. Robinson called soccer participant Crystal Dykes a bitch[.]
September 06—Mr. Robinson told a soccer participant (Crystal Dykes) she was too fat to play soccer.
September 06—Mr. Robinson told a soccer participant (Beryl Bannerman) that it was her fault her team had lost the game, at which point Beryl became upset and started crying.

October 06—Mrs. Robinson called club President and accused him of talking about her daughter Johnae, at that point Mrs. Robinson was told to refer all problems to club coordinator.

March 07—Mrs. Robinson accused coaches Neraida Benitez and Coreen Bullock of making sexual gestures in front of a van load of kids. . . .

April 07—Mrs. Robinson accused club president of being a racist[.]

April 07—Mrs. Robinson approached coach Benitez and told her she will listen to her and change her attitude (this incident occurred after Bureau Director ordered Mrs. Robinson to stay away from practices, and verbal communication from all Parks and Rec. staff, including coaches).

April 07—Mrs. Robinson called coach Benitez's home and stated her daughter Jacklyn was a whore, and that she is going to become pregnant soon if she didn't do something to control her.

July 07—Mr. Robinson called Club President and accused him of telling Kalina Jenkins, Andrea Rodrigues and Asia Bullock not to socialize with his daughter.

July 07—Mrs. Robinson called the home of Andrea Rodrigues and told her they were going to press charges on her for trying to drown her daughter at a soccer camp they attended at Lebanon Valley College.[53]

When the Robinsons were unable to have the soccer club suspension overturned, they filed the discrimination lawsuit in court alleging that Johnae would not have been suspended but for her mixed-race status and the interracial composition of her family. However, the Robinsons failed to proffer any evidence that Johnae's multiracial identity or her parents' interracial partnership motivated the decision to exclude Johnae from the soccer club. Indeed, the record was replete with nondiscriminatory justifications for excluding Johnae as a device for protecting the soccer club and its members from the over-the-top parental zealousness of the Robinsons, which the court characterized as "brash and unsportsmanlike."[54]

Nor did the Robinsons delineate how HSC club president Hicks's pregame rallying cry to "kick those white girls' butts" on the opposing team was itself discriminatory. Hicks's remark did not racially stereotype the opposing team. Hicks's remark did not refer to whiteness in a derogatory manner. Nevertheless, the court assumed for purposes of its analysis as to whether to dismiss the case that the comment was a racial remark. The Robinsons were thus accorded the benefit of having their interpretation of the remark as the benchmark against which to apply the public accommodations equality law. Notwithstanding the court's presumption that the comment was a racial remark, the court noted that one racial remark in isolation is insufficient to be considered tantamount to a discriminatory interference with the legal right to full and equal enjoyment of a public accommodation like the HSC facilities and services. As a result, the case was dismissed.

What might have been the legal analysis of Hicks's pregame remark had the case proceeded to trial? Absent an expression of animus against whiteness, stereotyped views about whites, or derogatory views about whites, analytically Hicks's remark is difficult to classify as definitively racist. What Hicks's remark did do was racially identify the opposing team. However, racial identification absent some action of differential treatment is not legally equivalent to discrimination. In other words, noticing another's racial appearance is not an unlawful act of discrimination itself. The noticing must be accompanied by adverse differential treatment.

Yet it is the very noticing of racial difference that the Robinsons appear to take issue with inasmuch as the noticing of whiteness was juxtaposed against Hicks's seeming presumption that his own team was nonwhite. The virulence of the Robinsons' reaction to Hicks's attempt to inspire team unity and confidence rooted in an identity as a nonwhite team would seem to underscore their central opposition to having their daughter presumed to be nonwhite. That appears to be at the heart of their violent reaction to the remark.

Yet, antidiscrimination law does not encompass personal affronts caused by others' presumption of nonwhite commonality. However, as chapter 6 shall explore, multiracial-identity proponents interpret slights to the particularity of personal multiracial identity as a form of racism while at the same time misapprehending the law's essential concern with hierarchical public discrimination. Chapter 6 thus expounds upon the consequences of the multiracial-identity definition of discrimination and the question of whether its fundamental concern is with pursuing a right to be viewed as race-less rather than articulating a unique mixed-race form of discrimination. Before doing so, chapter 5 examines one last set of case narratives raised in the criminal justice context.

5

Multiracial Discrimination in the Criminal Justice System

In our superficially more enlightened age, the phrase "mixed
race" has become the accepted term to describe people with
parents of different races. In fact the phrase has become a
tool of marketers and brand-conscious celebrities to suggest
whatever they're selling is all-inclusive, a living embodiment
of diversity. Many take great care in, for example, their Insta-
gram biographies to list their hyphenated backgrounds. But
there are limits to the term's utility.
—Nelson George, "Invisibly Black"[1]

When mixed-race persons are removed from society because they have
either been arrested or convicted of a criminal offense, the criminal justice system they enter is not devoid of racial hierarchy. In fact, there are
ways in which the criminal justice system is even more explicitly racially
stratified, with whites as the bulk of law enforcement officers and nonwhites as the disproportionate portion of arrestees and inmates. Ninety
percent of those admitted to prison for drug offenses in many states are
black and/or Latino, and convictions for drug offenses have been identified as the single most important cause of the explosion in incarceration
rates in the United States.[2] It is thus noteworthy to observe that mixed-
race arrestees and prisoners describe their experiences of discrimination
in ways that parallel the white versus nonwhite binary found in all other
multiracial discrimination contexts.

The petitions in this chapter of both inmates and arrestees alike
were brought pursuant to the civil rights statute, Title 42 USC § 1983.
Section 1983 enables claimants to assert civil claims (noncriminal law
claims) against state actors who deprive them of their constitutional

and federal law rights such as the Constitution's Fourteenth Amendment Equal Protection Clause sanction against racial discrimination, the Fourth Amendment's prohibition again unreasonable searches and seizures, or the Eighth Amendment's sanction against cruel and unusual punishment.

Interactions with Law Enforcement

Much of the racial-profiling literature details how even the most mundane of legal activities are viewed with great suspicion by law enforcement when engaged in by nonwhite persons.[3] Driving, shopping, standing in public places, and even entering one's own home are contested activities when engaged in by nonwhites. The cases that follow illustrate how this same pattern implicates multiracial persons as well. Indeed, prominent Black Lives Matter social movement activists for racial justice in the criminal justice context include multiracial persons such as Shaun King.[4]

At the same time, the criminal cases also demonstrate how courts do not deviate from established doctrine when multiracial persons claim being victimized by the criminal justice system. While criminal law and procedure have long been criticized for not properly attending to the racial bias that is infused into daily policing practices and into the way citizens form suspicions and report alleged crimes, the following cases do not evidence particular legal peculiarities deriving from the multiracial identity of the claimants.

Like Trayvon Martin, the black teenager who was shot dead in 2012 in Sanford, Florida, for looking suspicious by walking home in the rain with his hood on while holding a Skittles bag of candy, multiracial persons can also experience being viewed as inherently suspicious on the basis of their racial appearance like so many other countless nonwhites. The excessive force case of Brian and Derek Patterson against five white officers from the city of Akron police department is one such story.[5] Brian and Derek were brothers who were biracial and of African ancestry. They came home to Akron, Ohio, to visit their parents over the Memorial Day weekend in 2004. On the evening of May 27, 2004, the brothers met with friends at the Fat Tuesday Bar in downtown Akron, near the University of Akron. Patrons of Fat Tuesday and the neighboring bars often gather on the sidewalk to mingle and were doing so that evening as well. Approximately several hundred people were gathered together outside when the bars closed that evening.

Brian was sitting on the trunk of a police cruiser for several minutes when a police officer walked over and told him to get off his vehicle. Brian stood up without protest. After the officer walked away, Brian continued talking with a friend, and she testified that he then inadvertently leaned on the cruiser but did not sit on it. The friend further testified that after Brian just leaned against the police cruiser, the police "grabbed [Brian] up" and put his hands behind his back.[6] The officer instead testified that when he saw Brian leaning against the police cruiser, he told Brian to not even lean on the car and that he should leave the public area or risk going to jail, and when Brian refused to leave, the officer viewed his refusal as a "defensive posture" and thought Brian might be intoxicated and thus decided to arrest him.

When Brian's older brother, Derek, saw that two police officers were flanking Brian with his hands handcuffed behind him, Brian told him that he did not know why he was handcuffed. The police officer then allegedly yanked Brian by his left arm from the sidewalk into the street and tried to body slam him into the police cruiser. A predominantly white crowd of about ten to twelve people followed the officers to the driver's side of the cruiser and began shouting that the officers were racist and the words "police brutality."[7]

As Brian was being arrested, a crowd gathered and someone jumped on an officer, trying to intervene. Additional officers arrived and Brian was tased in the chest, and when he fell to the ground while still handcuffed, he was stunned several more times in the back, left leg, and buttocks. When Derek saw Brian being tased, he attempted to run to him and was tackled to the ground by an officer and was also tased five separate times after he was handcuffed. While the officers dispute the number of times they used their Taser guns on the brothers, a computer readout of the Taser gun corroborates the number alleged by the brothers.

For the brothers, a simple gathering with friends over a holiday weekend resulted in them being exposed to unprovoked police violence because their presence in the predominantly white space was interpreted as hostile from their "defensive posture."[8] The inherent police suspicion of the nonwhite body is unfortunately also evident in the case of these biracial brothers of African descent. Their mixed-race status neither diminished nor aggravated the commonality of their experience of the criminal justice system as racially biased.

When the brothers' excessive force claim went to trial, the judge refused to admit the Taser report corroborating their account. Upon appeal, the Sixth Circuit Court of Appeals concluded that the trial court had committed a reversible error in excluding the Taser report (because of the mistaken assertion that it was hearsay evidence).[9] The case was accordingly remanded for a new trial. Thereafter the parties entered into a settlement agreement, thereby making the brothers some of the very few litigants to garner success on an excessive force claim against the police. Their mixed-race status neither mitigated their exposure to racially informed excessive force nor did it interfere with their ability to use the law to redress their grievances.

While Brian and Derek's multiracial racialized criminal justice experience might be viewed as unique to them, the following story of an entire community of mixed-race persons treated as inherently criminal suggests that nonwhite stereotypes of criminality are systematically pervasive for mixed-race persons as well. Such was the case in the city of Alexandria, Louisiana, with its longstanding community of mixed-race persons of African and European descent who identify themselves as "Creoles of color."[10]

On February 5, 2006, Club Retro, a recently opened nightclub in Alexandria, Louisiana, was targeted for a preplanned, violent SWAT team raid.[11] Distinctive from the long-established club called GG's just one half-mile down the road, with its white owners and white clientele, Club Retro was owned by two nonwhite owners, Lyle and Dar, who identify with the Louisiana mixed-race term "Creole." Club Retro is also distinctive from club GG's white clientele, inasmuch as Club Retro serves a mixed-race clientele who come to see popular hip-hop artists performing at the club. GG's has never been raided in a manner similar to Club Retro.

When Club Retro was raided, the officers entered for the purposes of detecting the sale or possession of illegal narcotics, the sale of alcohol to minors, and fire code violations. Prior to the date of the raid, Club Retro had never been found to have violated the law in any way. The officers conceded that they did not have a warrant, probable cause, or exigent circumstances for entering the premises. They instead claimed that they entered the premises like any other member of the public and that they were conducting permissible administrative inspections. In the quest to discover whether any of the aforementioned administrative concerns were actually justified, the Rapides Parish deputy sheriffs descended upon the club without a warrant, and forty officers stormed the club with shotguns, AR-15 assault rifles, and pistols drawn and pointed at patrons and employees as the officers yelled racial epithets at them. As soon as the raid began, the deputy sheriffs seized, assaulted, battered, and handcuffed the club owners, Lyle and Dar.

Patrons were forced to the ground at gunpoint, and some alleged being hit with Taser guns by the officers. Because of the scale and ferocity of the raid, many of the employees thought that they were being robbed by armed gunmen. The officers destroyed property like mirrors and registers. As part of the search, some women were instructed to reach under their shirts, lift up their bras, and shake their breasts so that the deputy sheriffs could see if any illegal drugs would fall out. The officers detained the patrons and employees for approximately five hours and denied them access to the restrooms for so long that some patrons were forced to urinate in empty bottles, and one patron fainted.

The extremity of the officers' behavior did not stop with the patrons and employees. A deputy sheriff also broke down the door to a separate, private apartment that was inaccessible to the public and used as a residence for owner Lyle's minor child, a friend, and her babysitter. The sleeping children were forcibly removed from the apartment and the officer seated them at the bar in order to photograph them as if they were bar patrons. After bringing owner Lyle's minor child into the bar, the officers proceeded to arrest her mother, Erica, for endangering a child by permitting her to enter the establishment of an alcohol retailer. During the preliminary stages of the raid, the deputy sheriffs in charge addressed owner Lyle's wife, Erica, who is Caucasian, with the statement, "And you think you are white? You are not f——ing white."[12] After she was arrested, the officers threatened her with sexual assault. Lyle and Dar Doublet, the Creole owners of Club Retro, were also taken into custody.

As a result, Lyle and Dar filed a § 1983 civil rights action against several law enforcement officers, claiming, among other things, unlawful search and seizure, false arrest, and equal protection violations. The parallels between Lyle and Dar's interactions with the criminal justice system and the historically racialized treatment of monoracial-identified nonwhites also extend to how their equal protection claim was received by the court. The court found that the absence of any explicit officer statements that Club Retro was specifically targeted because it was "minority-owned and attracted a mixed-race and mixed-ethnicity crowd" thwarted the claimant's assertion that the officers had an intent to discriminate.[13] The fact that the club patrons were insulted with "profanities and racial slurs" was deemed immaterial to the question of discriminatory intent.[14] Furthermore, the fact that the neighboring white-owned club was never raided without probable cause or a warrant was considered by the court immaterial without any facts showing exactly how the white-owned club was similarly situated to Club Retro for purposes of comparison to demonstrate differential treatment.

In short, Lyle and Dar encountered the same challenges to proving a discrimination claim that all nonwhite claimants unfortunately encounter. Their status as mixed-race, Creole-identified claimants did not alter the ways in which all nonwhite claimants experience antidiscrimination law as imposing unrealistic demands for evidence of explicit statements regarding the intent to discriminate, and an obligation for an exacting comparison to a white equivalent alike in all factors to the claimant except for race. The officers raised the defense of qualified immunity for liability, which is a limited exemption from being sued. Qualified immunity can be accorded to government officials whose conduct does not violate clearly established statutory or constitutional rights of which a reasonable person would have known. The court thus permitted the officers to be shielded from being sued with respect to the Fourteenth Amendment equal protection claim.

In contrast to how the court allowed the officers to assert a defense of qualified immunity to the Fourteenth Amendment equal protection claim, the officers were not able to do so with respect to the Fourth Amendment unreasonable search and seizure acts of the warrantless SWAT raid and false arrest. The court found it particularly objectionable that the officers' raid was clearly just a fishing expedition and a guise "to discover evidence of criminal wrongdoing" rather than an appropriate intervention to halt criminal wrongdoing that they had probable cause to suspect was occurring.[15]

Lyle and Dar's mixed-race identity did not confound the court or lead it to misapply Fourth Amendment doctrine. The court recognized that Lyle and Dar had been subject to overzealous and inappropriate policing. This is a dynamic unfortunately quite familiar to so many other nonwhites as well.[16] However, unlike the vast majority of persons who assert claims of false arrest and unwarranted searches, Lyle and Dar were able to reach a settlement agreement with the accused officers. The extremity of the officers' bad conduct with respect to the unwarranted search and false arrests enabled Lyle and Dar to negotiate a settlement agreement.

Yet even when police officers appear to conduct themselves with the best of intentions, the racialized notions of those who report crimes, like our very own neighbors, can quickly ensnare innocent nonwhite persons in the criminal justice system. Harvard university professor Henry Louis Gates Jr. was certainly one of the most high-profile of nonwhites to experience this when a neighbor saw Gates attempting to enter his own home in 2009 and in alarm called the police for assistance about a black intruder committing a burglary in progress.[17] With the false accusation, the 911 call quickly escalated into an arrest of Gates for disorderly conduct after he tried to enter his own home. The parallel case of Charles Kowolonek, a biracial person of black and white ancestry, suggests that racial profiling by neighbors and others is an experience of discrimination that multiracial persons share with other nonwhites.[18]

Charles lived with his white mother in Florence, Kentucky. On August 22, 2007, Charles was playing with a soccer ball in the backyard when he accidentally kicked the ball through his mother's bedroom window, breaking the glass. Nervous about what his mother would say, Charles went to sit on the front porch to smoke a cigarette while his girlfriend went to get a broom to clean up the glass. A neighbor who heard the glass break and saw Charles walking in and out of the house made a 911 call to report a burglary by a "Puerto Rican" male.[19]

When the police officer arrived he found Charles seated on the front stoop of the house. The officer indicated that a burglary had been reported and asked him if he lived there and for his identification. Charles responded that he did live there but that he had "no clue" where to find his identification. The officer asked Charles twice to put down the cigarette he was attempting to light. When Charles refused to do so, the officer grabbed the cigarette from his mouth. The officer stated, "I'm not going to arrest you." However, when Charles turned his back on Moore to sit down again, the officer handcuffed his left wrist.

After his left wrist was cuffed, Charles reached for the screen door and grabbed it with his right hand. He claims he was attempting to stabilize himself. Miranda Wallace, Charles's girlfriend, then came from inside the house and tried to get between Charles and the police officer. Miranda explained that Charles lived there and that she would go inside to get Charles's mother or his identification. At about the same time, Charles let go of the door with his right hand, and the police officer and Charles found themselves in a mulched area near the stoop on the side of the house. Both men remained standing. Charles knew that the officer was trying to handcuff his other hand but would not allow the officer to do so because he was "embarrassed" about the police officer being in the yard. Instead, Charles held his arms taut at his side.

Four additional officers arrived shortly thereafter. The officers surrounded Charles and grabbed him, but Charles stood his ground. Amidst the commotion, Charles's mother began to yell from the upstairs window that Charles lived there. Charles heard one of the officers say that they were going to have to use their Tasers, and Charles told them that "a Taser would be the only way to get [me] . . . because my will was so high because of what—you know—I was at my house and my home . . ."[20] Charles testified that one of the officers then used his Taser on him. Subsequently, the officers fully handcuffed Charles and escorted him into a police cruiser. After the officers spoke with a few neighbors and with Charles's mother, they finally released him. Charles was held in the cruiser for about five minutes.

In assessing Charles's § 1983 claims for false arrest and excessive force, in violation of the Fourth Amendment, the court was persuaded that the neighbor's 911 call provided reasonable suspicion of a crime to justify restraining Charles. The court's analysis, while certainly unsatisfactory to Charles, was in fact an orthodox application of the legal doctrine that accords great weight to the existence of "reasonable" suspicion. Nothing about Charles's biracial identity altered the court's appraisal.

In short, the available case law suggests that multiracial persons can be targeted for police interrogation on the basis of their racial appearance, just as innumerable other nonwhites are on a daily basis. These case law findings also parallel the results from in-depth interviews where multiracial persons describe being targeted by law enforcement on the basis of their nonwhite racial appearances.[21] Stories of white police violence against multiracial persons also circulate in the news media.[22] Mixed-race identity does not seem to alter the influence of racialized stereotypes and implicit bias regarding the inherent criminality of those viewed as nonwhite. As with so many other antidiscrimination law contexts, the criminal justice system operates in a seemingly white-nonwhite binary that entangles people not on the basis of their personal identity but instead on the basis of their nonwhite appearance and/or knowledge about their nonwhite ancestry.

Life inside Correctional Facilities

The white versus nonwhite binary of the criminal justice system is particularly striking in the shift to the prison context, where prisons often operate with explicit norms of racial segregation despite Supreme Court case law that racially segregated prisons can compromise an inmate's equal protection racial equality rights.[23] Creating racialized prison spaces in order to control prison violence is not supposed to be tolerated unless absolutely needed for proper prison administration. However, preserving prison security is considered by the Supreme Court to be a compelling state interest that can sometimes justify racial segregation. This in effect permits many prisons to still structure racially segregated spaces along a white versus nonwhite continuum.[24] It is thus particularly noteworthy that the following multiracial claimants' narratives of white versus nonwhite discrimination are direct from the prisoners themselves filing their own claims without the benefit of legal representation. These are their unvarnished stories.

Jared M. Villery was a mixed-race Creole (African American and European person from Louisiana) who was incarcerated in the Kern Valley State Prison in California in 2007, when he was attacked by two white inmates as he crossed the prison yard.[25] They stabbed him in the back and repeatedly kicked and punched him. Because of prior racial assaults among the black and Hispanic inmates, only white inmates were permitted to use the yard, and Jared had asked not to be classified as white so as not to be endangered by the white inmates who did not want him among them.

Jared then proceeded to sue the California Department of Corrections for their deliberate indifference to his safety when they refused to "properly classify him as black" and thereby exposed him to cruel and unusual punishment in violation of the Eighth Amendment to the Constitution.[26] Because the prison had originally classified Jared as white and he had proceeded with the designation for the previous nineteen months of incarceration, the prison officials informed Jared that they would not change his official designation without some legal verification such as an original or certified copy of his birth certificate.

It may very well have been immaterial to Jared how he was racially classified before the prison became violently stratified by race. However, when white inmates were provided with an exclusive space to themselves, Jared clearly concluded that in the rigid white versus nonwhite structure that resulted, he needed to be classified as nonwhite in order to be segregated from the violence that could be meted out to nonwhites viewed as invading white spaces.[27] In short, Jared anticipated that within the rigidity of the prison racial divide, his nonwhite ancestry, however mixed, made him vulnerable to discriminatory violence. He was correct.

Unfortunately for Jared, the legal standard is high for making out an Eighth Amendment claim of cruel and unusual punishment.[28] Physical injury must be more than "de minimis," and his single attack in the prison yard was in the court's view an isolated incident insufficient to meet that standard.[29] As a result his case was dismissed.[30] One might certainly question the judicial characterization of a stabbing as "de minimis" simply because it occurred only once; however, that judicial conclusion cannot be attributed to a judicial misunderstanding of mixed-race identity and the law.

In direct contrast to the extraordinarily high threshold for proving an Eighth Amendment claim, prison administrators have a very low threshold for imposing housing segregation mandates as a presumed method for maintaining order in prisons. By relying upon the presumed racial bias of the prisoners to engage in racial violence, the prison administrators justify their norms of racially segregating the prisoners. Prison efforts to preserve racially restrictive spaces are so entrenched that they even override concerns with the danger of violence from housing rival gang members in the same space. Harvey Byrum Jr. was such a victim of a prison's fixation on racial segregation. Harvey was a mixed-race inmate of Hispanic descent at California Rehabilitation Center (CRC), a state prison in Norco, California, in which inmates were housed in sections according to race.[31]

When Harvey arrived at the facility in 2009 and was asked about any known gang affiliations, he stated that he was affiliated with the Northern Hispanics gang. The unnamed prison captain who interviewed Harvey indicated that she did not believe him and instead thought he should be housed with white inmates (seemingly because of his appearance). Harvey protested, asserting that he was of mixed race, and then showed her his Northern Hispanics gang tattoos. As there were no other Northern Hispanics gang members housed at CRC, the prison captain housed Harvey with inmates from the rival Southern Hispanics gang rather than deviate from the prison custom of race-based housing assignments. Harvey identified himself as mixed race, but for the prison captain all that was salient was his Hispanic ancestry. That Harvey was most endangered by fellow Hispanics from a rival gang was immaterial. All that mattered was the binary between white and nonwhite spaces.

On Harvey's first evening in the unit he was brutally attacked by six Hispanic inmates from the Southern Hispanics gang until he passed out and had to be hospitalized and segregated for thirty days to heal from his wounds. When the court requested that Harvey file an amended complaint to litigate his claim against the unnamed prison captain rather than the prison warden, who was not directly involved in the contested housing assignment, Harvey failed to follow up. After waiting five months for Harvey to continue litigating his claim, the court dismissed his case for failure to prosecute. It may well be that Harvey declined to continue litigating his claim because it also required that he first have filed a grievance with the prison administration directly and await their resolution before filing a claim in court.

The racial segregation that adversely affects multiracial inmates is not limited to the spaces in which they are required to sleep and exercise. Racial exclusion can also arise in the allocation of prison employment positions. John Willis Richard was a "Multiracial, Muslim" inmate of African descent at the Five Points Correctional Facility in Romulus, New York, who applied for and was denied employment in a section of the prison outside of his cell block in 2007.[32] No other inmate was restricted to employment in his cell block, and when John contested the denial of employment, Correctional Officer ("CO") Dignean stated, "[Y]ou're not going anywhere unless I say so, and I say no . . . your [sic] black right . . . Muslim or a five percenter . . . oh you're a mixed race mutt black."[33] John was also given the impression that CO Dignean hated him because he "allegedly killed a white man."[34] Thereafter, John was assigned to a lawns and grounds position within his cell block area and denied the opportunity offered to others of being placed on a waiting list for employment outside of his cell block area. John refused to take the lawns and grounds position and filed an internal grievance, at which point CO Tanea issued a disciplinary report and he was given ninety days of solitary confinement.[35]

When John filed his Fourteenth Amendment equal protection lawsuit, the court validated that he had sufficiently stated a legal claim based on his mixed-race status and religion, and thereby refused to dismiss his claim as requested by the prison authorities.[36] Moreover, the court mandated that the prison officials comply with John's request for "discovery" (that is, production of documents in their possession that could support John's case) or risk court sanctions. As this book went to press, the case was still pending and advancing towards trial.[37] The Fourteenth Amendment's equal protection demand for evidence of specific intent to discriminate is an exacting legal standard that foils many claimants.[38]

Even "race-neutral" prison spaces like prison libraries can be policed as racially exclusionary spaces at the discretion of biased correctional officers (COs). Michael Cannon had such an experience. Michael Cannon was a mixed-race inmate of African American ancestry at Stateville Correctional Center in Joliet, Illinois, who from 1997 to 1998 endured racial discrimination at the hands of a number of correctional officers, but from CO Burkybile in particular.[39]

When Michael attempted to use his law library privileges within the prison, CO Burkybile impeded his access while stating, "You are either a half-breed or of a mixed race and you shouldn't be up here. I hate all you half-breeds and you definitely won't be coming back to the law library this afternoon. I'll personally see to it and make sure you don't get back up in here."[40] When CO Burkybile next observed Michael attempting to enter the prison law library, he conducted a shakedown of Michael while allowing a white inmate to enter without being searched. During the search CO Burkybile confiscated a book about oral sex from Michael (that included photographs and thus was apparently deemed unauthorized pornography) because he was "the same half-breed he always hated." CO Burkybile continued to harass Michael with shakedowns, pointing a rifle at him and writing him false disciplinary tickets. In retaliation for the grievances that Michael filed against CO Burkybile, other COs withheld Michael's mail and razors, disrupted his Muslim prayer time, and denied his requests for toilet paper.

The judge found persuasive Michael's testimony and that of other inmates supporting his allegations of discrimination "on account of his mixed-race," and therefore denied the CO's request for dismissal of the case.[41] Especially significant was the judge's mandate that the parties enter into settlement negotiations, and the judge's providing Michael with a lawyer to represent him during the settlement negotiations. The case settled in 2003, and Michael received his requested transfer to the Hill Correctional Center.

Michael's is one of the few multiracial discrimination cases that multiracial-identity scholars applaud for a court acknowledging "animus as multiracial qua multiracial."[42] Yet what the multiracial-identity-scholar celebration of the case overlooks is the court's focus on how Michael was treated "less favorably than a similarly situated person of another race" when a white inmate was admitted to the prison law library without being searched, unlike Michael.[43] In fact, the court was quite emphatic that "in order to state an equal protection violation, [Michael] Cannon must assert that a state actor has treated him differently than persons of a different race and has done so intentionally."[44] In the court's search for such evidence of racial discrimination, the court compared the treatment Michael received as a "mixed race–part African-American" person to the treatment that white inmates received rather than all other monoracial inmates of other races.[45] The same binary analysis of a white versus nonwhite hierarchy prevalent in all the multiracial discrimination cases that the multiracial-identity scholars critique is also at work in Michael's case. The only difference is that the judge refers to Michael specifically as "mixed-race" throughout the written court opinions.

In short, the white versus nonwhite legal analysis across all the cases assessed in this book is the same, which suggests that at the heart of the multiracial-identity critique of contemporary antidiscrimination law is not its inability to resolve multiracial claims but rather many courts' failure to reference a mixed-race racial identity when referring to the claimants. In other words, the desire for a judicial reflection of the claimant's mixed-race personal identity is at the heart of the multiracial-identity scholar critique and not truly the inadequacy of antidiscrimination law. It is certainly the case that it would be preferable for judges to use the personal racial identity terms that claimants assert for themselves as a matter of courtesy. However, judges could be encouraged to do so without demanding that all of antidiscrimination law be overhauled. Why then do multiracial-identity scholars want antidiscrimination law reformed? The following chapter explores the essence of what motivates multiracial-identity scholars as a matter of Personal Racial Identity Equality.

6

Personal Racial Identity Equality

Multiracial consciousness [is] the next logical step in the
progression of civil rights.
—Reginald Daniel, *Racially Mixed People in America*[1]

What fundamentally concerns multiracial-identity scholars about multiracial discrimination cases despite the fact that the empirical record
does not by and large show anti-mixture animus nor a legal disfavoring
of multiracial claims? For multiracial-identity scholars, the primary locus
of multiracial discrimination is in any societal resistance to the assertion of multiracial identity. I call this approach to civil rights "Personal
Racial Identity Equality." It is epitomized by one legal scholar's notion that
"misrecognition of one's identity is social subordination."[2] One group of
psychologists similarly states that even asking mixed-raced people about
their racial ancestry is an instance of "overt racism" specifically "targeting
multiracial people."[3] These psychologists further aver that "not having a
[multiracial] racial designation on institutional forms is one of the most
invidious experiences of racism that occurs to multiracial people."[4]

The crux of the multiracial-identity-scholar critique of the antidiscrimination cases, then, is that the courts often reframe multiracial
complainants' self-identities by describing mixed-race complainants as
"monoracial" minority individuals.[5] Specifically, in many cases, courts
refer to mixed-race complainants as solely African American or black.[6]
These scholars take issue with this judicial characterization, arguing
that it conceals racial animus against multiracial individuals. Yet missing from the scholarly account is any specification as to how the judicial
oversimplification of the manner in which a claimant's race is described
has actually done violence to an individual's ability to form a more com-

plex identity or, more importantly, to the ability of a judge to appropriately assess the specific allegations of discrimination that are raised.

Antidiscrimination law compels judges to concentrate on how claimants are treated rather than how they personally identify. The empirical review of the cases shows that judges not only are focused on the allegations of how claimants are treated but also are often particularly solicitous of multiracial claims. The consideration accorded multiracial claims is reflected, first, in the judicial pattern of providing numerous extensions of time for claimants to file additional court documents rather than dismissing the claims for failure to prosecute. Second, particularly noteworthy is the judicial pattern of permitting many of the claims to be litigated rather than dismissed on the basis of defendant motions for summary judgment (as is so frequently done with discrimination cases).

The multiracial-identity-scholar privileging of personal racial identity is evident in Nancy Leong's concern with courts that "erase" multiracial identity and refer to multiracial complainants as simply black;[7] in Leora Eisenstadt's apprehension that the law currently forces "employees into an unnatural and uncomfortable identity";[8] and in Camille Gear Rich's proposal for an "elective race" ideological framework that provides a legal right to racial self-definition.[9] It also constitutes Tina Fernandes's and Scot Rives's insistence that a specific "multiracial" category be officially added to the list of protected racial groups that antidiscrimination law is presumed to implicitly recognize.[10]

The advocacy for specific inclusion of a multiracial category within antidiscrimination jurisprudence is curious when one considers that antidiscrimination statutes do not include any lists of specific racial groups. Rather, the statutes contemplate race broadly as social group–based differentiation. Thus all courts have also interpreted the statutes to include whites along with all other nonwhites for statutory protection. The few judges who mistakenly insist that a claimant's personal racial identity (whether monoracial or multiracial) exactly match the form of discrimination that is alleged to have occurred (such as insisting, for example, that a claimant who asserts a white personal identity cannot claim discrimination based on anti-black animus when an employer fires him or her after learning of his or her association with black friends) are clearly operating in contravention of the established legal doctrine, which does not mandate a match between a claimant's personal racial identity and the form of racial discrimination alleged.[11]

That multiracial-identity scholars focus on personal racial identity as the central issue of equality is part of the larger multiracial-social-movement preoccupation with identity. In fact, the academic treatment of multiracial identity is often very intertwined with the activism promoting recognition of a distinct multiracial identity on data collection forms.[12] It is perhaps the interest in multiracial activism that has led academics to disproportionately focus on the concern with expressions of personal racial identity.

For multiracial identity activists, the right to personal racial identity defines equality, as reflected in the "Bill of Rights for Racially Mixed People."[13] A bill of rights is traditionally understood to be a listing of legal rights provided the highest constitutional protection because they are understood to be fundamental rights of citizenship. It is thus quite notable that the central unifying item in the "Bill of Rights for Racially Mixed People" is the statement "I HAVE THE RIGHT To identify myself differently than strangers expect me to identify."[14] This is followed by the affirmations "I HAVE THE RIGHT To identify myself differently than how my parents identify me. To identify myself differently than my brothers and sisters. To identify myself differently in different situations," along with additional affirmations of a similar import.[15] The multiracial bill of rights is extensively reprinted and cited to within multiracial-identity circles and has become "something of a charter statement" and is often read at multiracial support group meetings.[16] However, the bill of rights and the racial-equality platform it advocates are focused "solely on naming and claiming a multiracial identity."[17] That is the totality of its civil rights concerns. Indeed, in Paul Spickard's examination of multiracial narratives, he notes that "almost no attention is paid to group needs. It is all about their own individual identity and relationship issues. . . . [T]heir multiracial claim is essentially an individualistic concern."[18] Habiba Ibrahim similarly describes it as an "individualist theory of justice."[19]

Multiracial-identity-movement survey responses concerning the nature of multiracial discrimination are equally narrow. Multiracial forms of discrimination that respondents articulate revolve around being questioned about their nonwhite personal identity.[20] Thus the "What are you?" question is often offered as emblematic of multiracial-specific discrimination.[21]

Being asked "What are you?" may create discomfort, but it has not been identified by multiracials as the agent of exclusion from opportunity. Perhaps this is why after sociologist Heather Dalmage participated in multiracial organizations and interviewed multiracial-identified people, she came to the conclusion that personal identity is paramount to multiracial communities because "they are not facing life-threatening persecution."[22] When questioned, multiracial respondents frequently report minimal experience with multiracial-specific discrimination.[23] Surveys of multiracial students indicate that they identify significantly fewer instances of discrimination than "monoracial" students.[24]

Moreover, at least one study suggests that phenotype and known black ancestry are stronger drivers of multiracial discrimination than actual mixed-race status, inasmuch as multiracials of black and Asian ancestry encounter more racism than multiracials of white and Asian ancestry.[25] This also parallels the greater rejection of black-white multiracial online date seekers as compared to Asian-white multiracials, and the greater resistance the public has to accepting multiracial identity when expressed by black-white multiracials as opposed to multiracials of other ancestries.[26] Multiracials of nonblack ancestry also receive greater social acceptance to assert a white racial identity with or without a cultural ethnic identity.[27] Significantly, the racial discrimination most frequently cited by multiracial people surveyed is that of being called a "monoracial" nonwhite racial slur.[28]

However, in sociologist Kimberly McClain DaCosta's interviews with multiracial activists (or what she interestingly calls "multiracial entrepreneurs"), each activist invoked civil rights as being at the root of his or her actions.[29] Yet, the multiracial activist agenda "has been limited to vague declarations that multiracial recognition could somehow help reduce racial strife."[30] When political scientist Kim Williams also interviewed every major leader of a multiracial-identity organization, she found that only 30 percent of the leaders reported that combating racism in their local communities was a priority for their group.[31]

Also notably absent has been any multiracial-activist examination of power in the consideration of what is racism.[32] African American studies scholar Jared Sexton describes this multiracial-activist dynamic as reducing the political to the personal.[33] The focus on personal identity is also evident in multiracial-identity Internet sites that discuss multiracial experiences but "do not challenge racism."[34] A significant deficit of the personal identity view of civil rights is its abstraction away from "articulating institutional forms of racism and the pervasiveness of white supremacy."[35]

This book's critique of Personal Racial Identity Equality therefore differs from popular attacks on "identity politics" that take issue with race-conscious questioning of racially exclusive institutions and racially segmented access to socioeconomic opportunity.[36] Personal Racial Identity Equality is thus problematic not because it centers itself on identity but rather because identity claims are isolated from material inequality concerns with social hierarchy and group-based disparities. In this way multiracial Personal Racial Identity Equality is distinctive from feminist articulations that the "personal is political." Feminism directly connects the unequal treatment of women in the private sphere with the subordination of women in the public sphere.[37] Similarly, the movement for transgender equality concerns itself with how bias against transgender identity leads to material deprivations in employment, mobility, and freedom from violence.[38] Recognition of transgender identity isolated from substantive group-based equality is not the goal. In contrast, Personal Racial Identity Equality takes a far narrower view of the importance of the personal by deifying personal identity as the primary objective in and of itself.

Another shortcoming of the Personal Racial Identity Equality view of civil rights is its presumption that the personal struggle with identity is unique to mixed-race persons. However, studies of "monoracial" identity formation indicate a level of complexity and contestation overlooked by the assumption that mixed-race identity formation is uniquely complex. For example, in the study of black racial identity, social psychologists note that the formation of black identity is contested and multidimensional[39] and more accurately viewed as a "metamorphic process" whereby individuals are not born black but "become Black."[40] The content of parental socialization has a significant effect on the formation of racial identity,[41] as does the environment in which a child is socialized.[42]

Exposure to institutional racial inequality also promotes black identity.[43] Adults who come to identify as black often characterize their early childhoods as untouched by any recognition of the social import of racial differences or the personal embrace of a black identity until a moment or moments of racial reckoning in which they are confronted with racial discrimination.[44] For example, early exposure to being called a "nigger" is often identified as the moment a person "learns" he or she is black.

The contested nature of racial identity continues into college, where, regardless of skin shade, African Americans can encounter the accusation of "Well, you're White. You're acting White now" based upon their behavior (or racial performance) being read as white.[45] Accusations of "acting white" and challenges to a person's authentic blackness can continue throughout life.[46] In short, black identity is a social process that is equally complex and fraught and thus not genetically preordained or simplified by appearing "monoracial." In fact, the research on black identity formation has undergone a number of transformations and is still evolving since its introduction in the 1970s to encompass the examination of multiple influences on racial identity.[47] Moreover, light-skinned African Americans, who can be perceived as racially ambiguous in much the same way multiracials describe, similarly articulate "not feeling Black enough."[48]

Nor is an individual's process of forming a racial or ethnic identification any less complex for those who come to identify themselves as Latino or Asian. For U.S. residents with familial and ancestral ties to a Latin American or Caribbean country, embracing Latino identity is a social process that is influenced by a great variety of factors such as generational level, English proficiency, skin shade, and socioeconomic status.[49] Moreover, studies show that the greater the personal experience of social exclusion, the higher the rates of adoption of a Latino or Hispanic identity.[50] Asian identity formation is similarly complex and multifaceted.[51] Like the Latino category, the Asian category is a collective panethnic term that is more readily embraced as a racial identifier the greater an individual's personal exposure to being racialized as an other.[52] In short, multiracial Personal Racial Identity Equality overstates the distinctive complexity of multiracial identity formation inasmuch as social science research indicates that racial identity formation is not static or preordained for other nonwhites.

The narrowness of the multiracial-activist Personal Racial Identity Equality agenda is embodied in its movement for a multiracial category on the decennial census and other data-collection forms. Most striking has been the failure to advance any substantive arguments regarding either a history of discrimination or a violation of the civil rights of multiracial people per se, which is a significant justification for including racial data in the census in the first place.[53] The census-category debate has focused instead on individuals' rights to choose their identity, rather than how multiracial status is treated within societal racial hierarchies. The census-category debate thus reveals the multiracial activists' constricted vision of civil rights.

For the past two decades, there has been a Multiracial Category Movement (MCM) by some racially mixed persons and their parents promoting the addition of a "multiracial" race category on the decennial census.[54] The stated aim of such a new category is to obtain a more specific count of the number of mixed-race persons in the United States and to have that tallying of mixed-race persons act as a barometer and promoter of racial harmony.[55] The MCM has targeted the census racial classifications in order to obtain "official recognition [of mixed-race Americans] as a distinct, powerful social unit."[56]

As proposed, a respondent could choose the "multiracial" box in lieu of the presently listed racial classifications of American Indian or Alaskan Native, Asian or Pacific Islander, Black, White, or Other. The census schedule also includes a separate Hispanic Origin ethnicity question. Except for the "Other" category, the aforementioned racial and ethnic classifications were instituted in 1978 by the U.S. Office of Management and Budget (OMB) in cooperation with the Minority Advisory Committee of the U.S. Census Bureau for standardized collection of racial data by the U.S. Bureau of the Census and all other federal government agencies.[57] The OMB director is authorized to dictate the methodology of all federal data collection forms.[58]

The intent of the instituted classification system is to meet the data collection obligations required by federal civil rights laws.[59] Specifically, census racial data is used to enforce the civil rights mandates against discrimination in employment,[60] in the selling and renting of homes,[61] and in the allocation of mortgages.[62] The U.S. Department of Housing and Urban Development also uses racial data to determine where to locate low-income and public housing.[63] Census racial data is also used in voting-rights redistricting to improve the political participation of people of color.[64] More importantly, with a decennial count of racialized social groups, one can detect patterns of exclusion by comparing the presence of a group in various spheres to its proportional representation in a community and the nation.

Although the Multiracial Category Movement (MCM) was unsuccessful in its effort to add a multiracial category to the 1990 census, it garnered significant support from racially conservative politicians such as Newt Gingrich.[65] In fact, the congressional subcommittee on Census, Statistics, and Postal Personnel was persuaded to hold a series of hearings in 1993 to explore the sufficiency of current racial classifications and the possible need for a multiracial category.[66] The OMB held hearings of its own one year later.[67] Thereafter, on October 29, 1997, the OMB adopted a federal Interagency Committee recommendation to reject the multiracial category in favor of the compromise of allowing individuals to check more than one racial category.[68]

Some MCM proponents are not satisfied with the OMB's decision, because multiple box checking does not directly promote a distinct multiracial identity. For instance, Project RACE president Susan Graham stated, "OMB is trying to erase 'multiracial' from the vocabulary."[69] These MCM proponents are committed to continuing the lobby for a multiracial category on future census forms.[70] Further, an OMB official has indicated that the issue of a multiracial category might be reconsidered with an increase in mixed-race persons.[71]

On the state level, the MCM has lobbied successfully for implementation of a multiracial category on local data-collection forms in Florida, Georgia, Illinois, Indiana, Michigan, and Ohio.[72] Additionally, similar legislation was proposed, but never enacted in Arizona, Maryland, Massachusetts, New Hampshire, Texas, Minnesota, New York, Oregon, Pennsylvania, Vermont, and Wisconsin.[73] On its own initiative, Harvard University's applications for admission included a multiracial category for the 1992–1993 academic year.[74] Since then the Harvard application has returned to listing only the traditional census racial categories along with inviting applicants to check as many races as apply, following the model of the Common App used by most colleges.[75]

Yet, the significance of the MCM extends beyond the actual decision of how mixed-race persons should be counted. What is most salient is how the struggles over the census racial categories have fostered a discourse of exalting personal racial identity and characterizing any incursions on expressions of personal identity as a civil rights issue in and of itself absent any mixed-race-specific material inequality.

Some might suggest that the multiracial-promoted Personal Racial Identity Equality exaltation of identity as a civil rights issue is not necessarily incompatible with the traditional civil rights group–based material inequality approach to civil rights. Yet the concept of Personal Racial

Identity Equality is not innocuous when it interferes with the ability to identify and address the material inequality that individuals are exposed to apart from their personal identity. Indeed, there is a harmful disconnect between the multiracial-identity-scholar critique of antidiscrimination law and the actual demonstrated adequacy of the laws to address multiracial discrimination.

The disconnect evidences itself in a number of ways: first in how the vast majority of multiracial discrimination claimants articulate a binary pattern of white versus nonwhite allegations of discrimination rather than filing allegations rooted in actual anti-mixture bias; second in how the cases show courts appropriately enforcing antidiscrimination law; and finally in how courts appropriately administer the few claims with actual anti-mixture allegations. Antidiscrimination law is capacious enough to handle multiracial claims. In short, the close examination of these claims undercuts the multiracial-identity-scholar critique of the cases as exhibiting judicial confusion about anti-mixture bias and the inadequacy of antidiscrimination law.

This multiracial-identity-scholar disconnect from the reality of the cases likely stems from the primacy that these scholars place upon the recognition of personal identity above all else, which in turn clouds their ability to appreciate the adequacy of the judicial enforcement of the cases that instead focuses on the harms of group-based racial hierarchies. The emphasis on the recognition of personal racial identity is a prominent feature of the public activism for cultural recognition of a multiracial identity that is a misplaced import into the legal context. When the personal identity focus of the multiracial social movement is transplanted into the legal context, it obstructs the ability to understand the needs of multiracial victims of discrimination, whose disadvantage clearly flows from white versus nonwhite group-based racial hierarchies. This disserves the needs of multiracial persons experiencing discrimination. Moreover, the rhetoric of Personal Racial Identity Equality has come to be used to undermine the enforcement of antidiscrimination law, as will be discussed in the next section.

Rhetoric Has Consequences: Supreme Court Considerations of
Personal Racial Identity Equality

We have to guard against the rhetoric of equality used by
those who feign disapproval of racism while they reassert
white privilege and white supremacy.
—Deborah Waire Post, "The Salience of Race"[76]

In direct contravention to the multiracial identity movement pursuit of
racial identity recognition as a civil rights issue, contemporary affirmative action opponents have drawn upon the lobby for multiracial identity
as a justification for invalidating policies of racial inclusion. Starting
with the 2003 oral arguments before the Supreme Court in the companion University of Michigan affirmative action cases of *Gratz v. Bollinger*
and *Grutter v. Bollinger*, the lawyers challenging the constitutionality of
affirmative action drew upon the existence of mixed-race persons to
bolster their arguments. In the challenge to the University of Michigan
law school's affirmative action policy, the petitioner's attorney stated in
his Supreme Court oral argument that "[i]t is precisely because we are a
nation teeming with different races and ethnicities—one that is increasingly interracial, multiracial, that it is so crucial for our Government to
honor its solemn obligation to treat all members of our society equally
without preferring some individuals over others."[77] In the challenge to
the University of Michigan's undergraduate affirmative action policy, the
petitioner's attorney asserted during his Supreme Court oral argument
that no policy of affirmative action could be constitutional that relied
upon a candidate's self-assertion of racial identity when a mixed-race
applicant might choose to identify with a multiplicity of backgrounds.[78]
In the petitioner's view, the mere existence of mixed-race applicants
underscores how "standardless" and thus unconstitutional affirmative
action is.

The Supreme Court ultimately rejected the University of Michigan's
undergraduate point-system version of affirmative action, which allo-

cated a fixed number of points for the diversity of an applicant's background. The diversity-related points were added to the portfolio of points, which included standardized testing and high school grades. The Court ruled that this point system was too "mechanistic" and thus amounted to a quota. In contrast, the Court decided that affirmative action was constitutional when race was only one factor among many in a holistic consideration of an applicant's background and talents, as was the case with the University of Michigan's law school policy, which the Court did approve.

The oral arguments are noteworthy for signaling the trend of using multiracial identity to challenge policies of racial inclusion in affirmative action litigation. This is a trend that has gotten stronger with the passage of time and the increasingly vehement opposition to affirmative action, a criticism emboldened by Justice O'Connor's statement in the *Grutter* decision that "[w]e expect that 25 years from now, the use of racial preferences will no longer be necessary to further the interest approved today."[79]

Ten years after the decisions in *Grutter* and *Gratz*, Supreme Court Chief Justice Roberts directly posed questions regarding the implication of mixed-race candidates for affirmative action programs, in a 2013 case challenging the University of Texas's consideration of race in its affirmative action plan. In *Fisher v. Texas* (*Fisher I*), the Court affirmed the process of considering race as a factor among others in a public university's admissions efforts to achieve a more diverse student body.[80] But the Court also narrowed the ability to use affirmative action by stating that in the judicial assessment of whether a particular admissions policy satisfies the strict scrutiny standard of being narrowly tailored in pursuit of the goal of diversity, the university is not entitled to deference or a presumption of good faith in its operation of its programs.

In the oral arguments for *Fisher I*, Justice Roberts questioned how compelling the university pursuit of a diverse student body could be if a candidate who was "one-quarter Hispanic" or "one-eighth Hispanic" is allowed to identify on the admissions application as Hispanic without the university verifying the veracity of the racial identification.[81] For Justice Roberts, mixed-race applicants are a cause for generating skepticism about the integrity and ability of affirmative action to truly achieve racial diversity.

Nor is this skepticism limited to Justice Roberts. When the Supreme Court reexamined the University of Texas (UT) affirmative action policy in *Fisher II*, two other Supreme Court justices joined Roberts in raising concerns about the viability of affirmative action in light of multiracial-identified applicants. These concerns were included in the text of their joint opinion dissenting from the majority decision that the race-conscious admissions program in use at UT is lawful under the Equal Protection Clause of the Constitution. In *Fisher II*, Justices Alito, Roberts, and Thomas joined in a dissenting opinion that opined that the affirmative action program was faulty because "as racial and ethnic prejudice recedes, more and more students will have parents (or grandparents) who fall into more than one of UT's five [enumerated racial] groups."[82] This presumption that the increase in multiracial-identified applicants undermines both the implementation and justification for affirmative action did not originate with the justices. As with the *Grutter* and *Gratz* litigation in Michigan a decade earlier, the challenge to UT's affirmative action program was replete with opposition papers referencing the presumed significance of a mixed-race applicant pool.

Worthy of mention are three different *amicus curiae* briefs (a "friend of the court" legal pleading submitted by an entity or person who is not a party to the lawsuit but wishes to share pertinent information with the court). Each of these *amicus curiae* briefs opposed affirmative action and justified its position with references to mixed-race applicants. Specifically, the American Center for Law and Justice's *amicus curiae* brief referenced the many "websites devoted to identifying and celebrating multiracial children" and their claims that "multiracial Americans are one of the fastest growing populations in the country . . . [a]nd in a hundred years . . . could well become America's majority."[83] On the basis of these claims about multiracial identity, the brief concludes that affirmative action programs will become impossible to implement. Similarly, the Judicial Watch, Inc., and Allied Educational Foundation briefs situate their opposition to affirmative action in part on the basis of the difficulty of applying race-conscious programs to mixed-race applicants who do not neatly fit mutually exclusive racial categories.[84] The same presumptions are invoked in the joint *amicus curiae* brief of the Pacific Legal Foundation, Center for Equal Opportunity, American Civil Rights Institute, Project 21, National Association of Scholars, Individual Rights Foundation, and Reason Foundation.[85]

What each of the foregoing examples demonstrates is the influence that multiracial-identity discourse has had on justifying challenges to policies of racial inclusion even in cases where the Supreme Court has endorsed the constitutionality of affirmative action while at the same time imposing constraints on its use. Especially alarming, then, is the Supreme Court's reference once again to mixed-race persons in its decision authorizing outright state bans on affirmative action. Over two decades of multiracial discourse situating mixed-race persons as racially unique and emblematic of racial progress has bolstered the opposition to policies of racial inclusion and provided such opponents additional fodder for their argumentation. Rhetoric has consequences.

In *Schuette v. Coalition to Defend Affirmative Action*, the Court held that a public ballot–initiated amendment to the Michigan State Constitution that bans the use of affirmative action at public universities is not a state action that inflicts injury on racial minorities in violation of the Equal Protection Clause of the United States Constitution.[86] In doing so, the Supreme Court gave license to any other state to ban race-based affirmative action as well. Seven states currently ban race-based affirmative action at all public universities. California, Washington, Michigan, Nebraska, Arizona, and Oklahoma all passed bans through voter referendums. In Florida, Governor Jeb Bush issued an executive order creating the ban.[87] Colorado proposed a ban that was narrowly defeated in 2008.[88]

In assessing whether the ballot initiative in *Schuette* was intended to harm racial minorities, Justice Kennedy asserted in the Court opinion that "in a society in which those [racial] lines are becoming more blurred, the attempt to define race based categories also raises serious questions of its own."[89] In other words, the growth of multiracial-identified persons calls into question the utility of presuming that individuals have a predetermined perspective about being harmed or not by the ballot initiative on the basis of their racial identity.

Justice Scalia elaborates further on this theme in his concurring opinion in the case. For Justice Scalia, making any assumptions about how racialized group members perceive race-based policies like affirmative action bans that might impede their access to traditionally racially exclusive institutions is itself an exercise that "promotes the noxious fiction that, knowing only a person's color or ethnicity, we can be sure that he has a predetermined set of policy 'interests' thus reinforcing the perception that members of the same racial group—regardless of their age, education, economic status, or the community in which they live—think alike [and] share the same political interests."[90] To underscore his point, Scalia then poses the question, "Does a half-Latino, half-American Indian have Latino interests, American-Indian interests, both, half of both?"[91] At first blush it may appear like a simple matter of logic for Justice Kennedy and Justice Scalia to equate assertions of which political actions do and do not harm a racial group with impermissible stereotyping.

However, the justices' leveraging of multiracial identity to question race-conscious analysis overlooks two important factors. First, histories of racial discrimination have been found to influence nonwhite attitudes towards race policy issues like affirmative action. For instance, one study of biracial political attitudes indicates that respondents who identified as biracial (white-black) joined "monoracial" blacks in holding more supportive views of affirmative action and other matters explicitly racial in nature than "monoracial" white respondents.[92] Hence, from the perspective of race-based politics, there is such a thing as a group-based racial viewpoint that does not diminish simply because a nonwhite group member is racially mixed.

Secondly, the Court also overlooks the extent to which racial harms can be imposed on group members regardless of the diversity of their perspectives. Racialized group members can certainly have a diverse array of political perspectives about any given topic, including affirmative action, but still suffer a common group-based harm or disadvantage with respect to their access to traditionally racially exclusive institutions absent affirmative action in a manner that is ultimately harmful. Numerous studies show that with the advent of affirmative action policies, there was a dramatic change in the U.S. labor market, with a demonstrated increase in the numbers of racial minorities in almost every job niche.[93] There is near-unanimous consensus among economists that such programs of inclusion contributed to the improved income levels of racial minorities.[94] Moreover, affirmative action policies have increased the racial and ethnic diversity of many educational settings. Ballot initiatives that ban affirmative action therefore hinder the inclusion of racial minorities in ways that can directly harm them regardless of how they racially identify themselves.[95] As is the case with the multiracial discrimination cases examined in this book, racial mixture does not diminish the extent of harm that a ballot initiative can cause. The empirical data indicates that after various state affirmative action bans were instituted, the numbers of racial-minority admissions were substantially reduced.[96]

Multiracial applicants are vulnerable to being harmed by affirmative action bans.[97] For example, at Rice University the admission rate for multiracial applicants has risen to approximately 23 percent at the same time that the admission rate for the freshman class as a whole is approximately 19 percent.[98] Multiracial students at Rice now account for about 6 percent of the freshman class, which is nearly as many as those who solely identify themselves as black or African American, and more than double the proportion of persons who identify with multiple races on the national census.

On a national level, there is some indication that multiracials with African ancestry in particular are significantly overrepresented among black students at selective higher education institutions.[99] A 2007 survey of college freshmen who entered the thirty-one elite colleges and universities comprising the Consortium on Financing Higher Education revealed that 19 percent of black students were "Black Multiracials." The claim that "Black Multiracials" are overrepresented on college campuses emanates from the comparison to the census data showing that mixed-race blacks only constitute 8.4 percent of the black population under eighteen, and 2 percent of those who are sixty-five years or older.[100] In addition, an earlier 1999 study of twenty-eight selective colleges and universities demonstrated that multiracials of African ancestry and black immigrants made up 41 percent of black freshmen.[101] Some universities particularly stand out for the high proportion of their multiracial student population. At Yale University, 54 percent of the black students enrolled in the freshman class of 2014 were multiracial.[102]

This empirical data refutes the inferences drawn from one team of social psychologists in a study of less than two hundred undergraduate students in which the students rated hypothetical biracial college applicants as "less warm" than single-race-identified applicants.[103] The study presumed that being viewed as "less warm" would hinder the college admission of multiracial applicants. While the sample of undergraduate study participants may have displayed negative attitudes about multiracial applicants, admissions data suggests that actual adult admissions officers are much more favorably inclined and that multiracial applicants are benefited by affirmative action programs. The attitudes of undergraduate college student participants in other studies were similarly nonreflective of how receptive actual admissions officers are to multiracial applicants.[104] Interview data with admissions officers also suggests that a number of admissions officers at very selective colleges view multiracial applicants as helpful at addressing the lack of diversity of whichever portion of their ancestry is most underrepresented at the college.[105] This course of action in effect favors the admission of multiracial candidates, undermining the notion that multiracial identity penalizes applicants.

Nevertheless, multiracial-identity scholars have raised a concern with admissions officers focusing on what they term "the least represented portion" of a multiracial applicant's ancestry, meaning the nonwhite ancestry. The concern is that "such practices *minoritize* multiracial students by imposing racial identity, [and] foreclosing the possibility of more nuanced self-identification."[106] However, this misgiving about multiracials being "minoritized" conflates the civil rights integration objectives of affirmative action with an individual's freedom to form a personal identity. The actions of admissions officers have no bearing on how each applicant personally identifies or lives his or her life.

Standing alone, the objection to being "minoritized" is an attempt to divorce nonwhite ancestry from the societal derogation that is often attributed to it. As Deborah Waire Post notes, "The idea that we are all 'people of color' does not sit comfortably with many people who are denominated 'minorities' by the dominant culture."[107] However, the antidiscrimination cases examined in this book illustrate the reality of multiracial status being viewed as nonwhite and disparaged accordingly regardless of an individual's personal identity. These findings are corroborated by related studies of identity and discrimination.

In a psychological study of respondent reactions to persons with racially ambiguous appearances, the psychologists found that when respondents were told that a person had mixed-race ancestry, the respondents then reflexively categorized the individual as nonwhite.[108] The psychologists go on to note that conveying mixed-race ancestry may serve to make the socially subordinate aspect of a person's ancestry most salient in ways that activate stereotyping and ensuing experiences of prejudice and discrimination. Similarly, a sociological study of Dominican and Puerto Rican migrants in New York City found that a nonwhite appearance was more predictive of discrimination than the respondents' varying personal mixed-race racial identities.[109]

Moreover, severing notions of nonwhiteness from an understanding about its subordinated societal status runs completely contrary to the aims of affirmative action. Historically, affirmative action has been understood as a system designed to remedy past discrimination and eliminate current and future discrimination by integrating racially exclusive institutions and providing an opportunity for upward mobility. When admissions officers consider whether an applicant's background reflects an underrepresented demographic at the university, they do so as a means to racially integrate the institution and provide opportunity. While Supreme Court jurisprudence has narrowed the constitutional basis upon which an affirmative action program can be held valid so that only the pursuit of "diversity" is discussed in contemporary affirmative action cases, in practice educational institutions have a much broader mission in their consideration of race that can incorporate concerns with advancing social equality.[110] Multiracial applicants with ancestry that society views pejoratively are well served by an evaluation practice that seeks to be more racially inclusive. An admissions focus on the underrepresented portions of an applicant's background does not transform a multiracial candidate into a minority. The focus on nonwhiteness simply reflects the societal views about nonwhiteness that affirmative action seeks to address by integrating spheres of opportunity.

However, this does not mean that fluid racial identity or any other aspect of personal identity is unimportant in the college admissions process. The whole purpose of the college admission essay is to inform admissions officers about as many aspects of an applicant's personal identity as the applicant wishes to share. One study of college applicant essays submitted to the University of Michigan during the fall 2004 admissions cycle found that the "diversity question essay" responses by and large exhibited a broad-based array of topics, with expansive notions of diversity that incorporated many nonracial factors.[111] In short, the affirmative action civil rights agenda focus on the public meaning of race is not mutually exclusive from the ability to fully express personal identity. In this way, the college admission context usefully illustrates the value of analytically distinguishing between the expression of personal identity and the civil rights focus on group-based racial realities.

Consequently, the next chapter will offer a "socio-political race" proposal for analyzing matters of discrimination that is meant to replace the personal racial identity perspective relied upon by multiracial-identity scholars. The "socio-political race" concept acknowledges the function of personal racial identity while at the same time providing a more effective tool for assessing racism and pursuing equality. With a "socio-political race" approach, civil rights activists will be better poised to stem the last ten years of challenges to race-based affirmative action, which are based upon the conjecture that the growth of mixed-race persons undercuts the legitimacy of affirmative action policies. Because the Supreme Court affirmative action litigation references to mixed-race persons has paralleled the public discourse notion that the growth of multiracial-identified persons signals the decline of racism, only a direct challenge to the personal racial identity equality perspective relied upon by multiracial-identity scholars has the potential to more effectively pursue racial equality.

7

The Way Forward

The Socio-political Race Approach

> Personal identity and personal choice are relevant issues,
> but they are subsidiary to questions of race, racism, and the
> structures of racial oppression.
> —Minkah Makalani, "A Biracial Identity or a New Race?"[1]

What this book's review of multiracial discrimination cases has revealed is, first, that multiracial claimants are not legally disadvantaged in raising claims of discrimination with our present civil rights laws. Secondly, the cases demonstrate the enduring power of white privilege and the continued societal problem with nonwhiteness in any form. Specifically, the cases illustrate the perspective that nonwhiteness taints rather than the notion that racial mixture itself is problematic. In the rare cases where racial mixture is directly targeted, traditional civil rights law has been properly applied. Yet this insight is lost in the midst of the multiracial-identity scholars' singular focus on promoting mixed-race identity.

Multiracial victims of discrimination will be better served by legal analyses that seek to elucidate the continued operation of white supremacy that harms multiracials as nonwhites. Such a focus will also better support all antidiscrimination law and public policies that, as was shown in the previous chapter, are now being in part challenged on the premise of multiracial exceptionality. The key antidote to such an erosion of civil rights is a theoretical grounding that shifts away from a focus on personal individual identity recognition to a focus on group-based racial realities.[2]

While multiracial-identity scholars assert that antidiscrimination principles necessitate the protection of the expression of personal fluid racial identity, this position loses sight of antidiscrimination law's foundational distinction between the personal and the private. Tarunabh Khaitan explains that globally, discrimination law maintains a divide between the public and private in which the legal duty not to discriminate is only imposed upon persons and institutions that interact with the public and are in a position to grant or deny access to goods or services.[3] Such public duty bearers include the state, employers, landlords, hotels, restaurants, and other service providers. While private individuals may certainly harbor prejudices and even make decisions based upon those prejudices, the legal duty not to discriminate does not include them. Antidiscrimination law focuses upon public duty bearers because of their power as gatekeepers of opportunities, basic goods, and social mobility. Private individuals acting outside of public spheres do not have the same potential for influencing societal opportunity. Khaitan provides the following example: "[A] consumer who refuses to shop at a store simply because its proprietor is Muslim has probably not violated any law, even though most people would condemn such refusal as discriminatory. The law does not require us to refrain from discriminating on the ground of race in the choice of our friends either."[4] This is why antidiscrimination law is unidirectional in nature. Employees are not prohibited from holding racial bias against their employers. Nor are tenants and consumers regulated in expressing racial bias, however odious those expressions may be. The liberty right to hold bias along with a plethora of other perspectives and opinions is sustained until it materially encroaches on another's access to public goods. In other words, antidiscrimination law's primary concern is with public effects and not personal expressions of bias. For this reason, legal scholar Lauren Sudeall Lucas also concludes that conflating the personal need for identity formation with the role of law in addressing group-based discrimination risks harming U.S. constitutional equal protection equality enforcement.[5]

Hence multiracial-identity scholar Camille Gear Rich's expansive concern with privileging a "right to self-definition" may be well-intentioned in its desire to maximize the liberty interests of those with fluid racial identities, but it misapprehends the ultimate purpose of antidiscrimination law.[6] Extending Khaitan's analysis of the function of antidiscrimination law to the multiracial context illuminates how personal racial identity may be important to an individual but not salient to the public concerns of antidiscrimination law, unless a public duty bearer has denied or altered access to a public good on the basis of that racial identity.

This does not mean that all expressions of personal identity are irrelevant to antidiscrimination law. The key is the effect of biased action on the access to public goods. Thus, when the expression of personal racial identity is penalized with an interference in the access to a public good, antidiscrimination law is justified in regulating the discriminatory behavior. This is why Devon Carbado's and Mitu Gulati's work about how distinct "racial performances" in the workplace elicit varied responses is directly tied to an employee who suffers disparate treatment.[7] The concept of racial performance focuses on how nonbiological factors such as the manner in which one speaks, styles one's hair, makes wardrobe choices, and aligns with particular cultural expressions in music, dance, and otherwise all influence the way others perceive one's racial appearance and react to it. The idea of racial performance is thus based upon the volitional choices an individual can make to express his or her racial identity.

While multiracial-identity scholars often cite to Carbado and Gulati's work on racial performance to support their emphasis on personal racial identity expression, they frequently lose sight of Carbado and Gulati's theoretical grounding in antidiscrimination law's foundational concern with public differential treatment. For Carbado and Gulati, racial performance matters to law only insofar as it is used to deny a racialized group member access to opportunity and services. They underscore this with their example of Mary, a black woman who has been denied a work promotion despite her excellent work record and educational background.[8] While other black women in the office are promoted, Mary is not. It also happens that Mary is the one black woman who styles her hair in dreadlocks and wears West African–influenced attire on Casual Fridays in ways that the supervisors may unconsciously find nonconforming and threatening. Racial performance theory is not concerned with the specifics of any particular personal identity racial performance, but rather with having antidiscrimination law sanction employers and others who deny a public good like a work promotion because of racialized concerns with that performance. The material inequality that results from the denial of public goods is at the center of Carbado and Gulati's discussion of racial performance.

The multiracial-identity-scholar preference is to isolate a claimant's personal identity concern with perceived harm to dignity from the question of material inequality. For instance, Camille Gear Rich urges that U.S. antidiscrimination law "attend to the dignity concerns of individuals as they attempt to control the terms on which their bodies are assigned racial meaning."[9] What the demand for a dignity-focused approach to antidiscrimination law overlooks is how inequality includes indignity but is not reducible to it.[10] "It is just not all there is to it, or even its irreducible core, sine qua non, or floor."[11] For this reason a dignity-focused approach cannot substitute for the harm of inequality on its own terms. As legal scholar Catharine MacKinnon explains,

> Inequality is always undignified. But reducing its injury to the feeling of indignity in the subordinated person makes it all mental and within the unequally treated person, which tends to cover up, even trivialize, the coercive and injurious external conditions and systemic acts usually involved, the material deprivations and physical harms inflicted by dominant groups, along with the resources and status they benefit from. . . . [Inequality's] demeaning meanings cannot be ended without also ending its material deprivations. For instance, the harm of unequal pay is not only that it deprives one of dignity, although it can, but that it deprives one of money. Reducing inequality to its dignitary dimension misses too much to be able upon remediation to produce equality.[12]

In short, a dignity-focused approach to discrimination sidelines the concern with material inequality, which is the only effective mechanism for addressing racial subordination inasmuch as inequality is always about material hierarchy. Most importantly,

> the inequality exists whether the person subjected to it experiences a loss of dignity or not. Put another way, dignity is a value or feeling. Equality is only secondarily a value or feeling. Primarily it is a fact. Inequality is also a fact. . . . The injury of inequality is not reducible to feeling bad at its indignity, although we often do. The injury is the harm of the fact of one's equal humanity being denied realization in the world. Fixing the world will fix the way we feel about it.[13]

Applying Catharine MacKinnon's substantive equality theory insights about the weaknesses of the dignity-focused approach to the context of multiracial discrimination illuminates the mistake of equating the feeling of being disgruntled by any resistance to multiracial identity with antidiscrimination law's fundamental concern with material inequality. Indeed, even *Brown v. Board of Education*'s stated concern with "generating inferiority in the hearts and minds" of schoolchildren was rooted in the material inequality of racially segregated public education rather than its harm to dignity.[14] This is underscored by *Brown*'s focus on material harm to black children rather than any speculation that the "hearts and minds" of white children would perceive any racial inferiority from being separated from black children.[15] The premium placed by multiracial-identity scholars on the pursuit of a dignity claim for recognition of a personal racial identity overlooks the intrinsic concern with material inequality that is fundamental to antidiscrimination law. As the Supreme Court case law in the higher education affirmative action context discussed in the previous chapter indicates, judicial preoccupation with protecting individual dignity in fact endangers the enforcement of antidiscrimination law. The erosion of antidiscrimination law is also evident in the Supreme Court's decision to forbid public K–12 schools from pursuing racial diversity by directly employing a racial balancing policy when selecting students.[16]

In 2007, the Court in *Parents Involved in Community Schools v. Seattle School District No. 1* held that voluntary integration programs that are not seeking to address historic intentional discrimination cannot use race in a mechanistic way to determine where pupils are assigned to public schools. The decision rejected what it called racial balancing for its own sake, along with the notion that K–12 schools should have the prerogative to institute plans to maintain racial diversity. The Court focused on how "one of the principal reasons race is treated as a forbidden classification is that it demeans the dignity and worth of a person."[17] Immaterial to the Court in *Parents Involved* are the demonstrated harms that come from allowing a school to become racially exclusive in a society that continues to accord hierarchical meaning across racial groups. Hence, in practice, the judicial consideration of personal dignity harms in the racial context has not always been conducive to the pursuit of the greater racial equality that multiracial-identified scholars and others actually seek.

Moreover, the personal racial identity dignity focus has also propelled significant legislative threats to the continued enforcement of antidiscrimination. Opponents of policies of racial inclusion have also been at the forefront of lobbying for the abolition of any state collection of racial and ethnic statistics under the purview of so-called racial privacy initiatives.[18] The premise of "racial privacy" initiatives is that racial and ethnic identity is exclusively a personal matter that should be of no concern to the state, even to fulfill its goal of eradicating racism. However, racial and ethnic statistics enable the government and social justice activists to better enforce our nation's antidiscrimination laws by being able to identify groupwide patterns of racial exclusion. In contrast, social justice activists from countries that do not collect racial ethnic statistics (such as France and several Latin American countries) consistently report how it hinders their ability to monitor and address racial discrimination.[19]

Notwithstanding the important role of governmental racial data in monitoring racial inequality, a large number of multiracial advocacy organizations publicly endorsed the "racial privacy" initiatives.[20] Thus

THE WAY FORWARD | 117

far the legislative "racial privacy" initiatives have not been successful in interfering with the important civil rights tool of gathering racial data, but its proponents have vowed to continue with their efforts. Moreover, its proponents have most recently been urging the U.S. Census Bureau to abolish the collection of racial data on the decennial census.[21] Should the "racial privacy" lobby garner any inroads in its effort to make racial identity treated as exclusively a personal matter, the injury to civil rights law will be significant. As Chris Chambers Goodman astutely observes,

> When Harry Potter covers himself with the invisibility cloak, he still acts, reacts, and causes results, while those around him simply cannot see what he is doing. If racial privacy legislation succeeds in covering racial and ethnic statistics with a similar cloak, people still will act (discriminate), react (retaliate), and cause results (racial harm), but litigants will not be able to prove those actions, nor link their results to the actors, thus subverting the enforcement of civil rights laws.[22]

Therefore, this book seeks to propose an intervention to counter the multiracial-identity-scholar disproportionate emphasis on a personal racial identity perspective that misapprehends the social-political significance of race in the assessment of equality problems. The proposal is for an explicit "socio-political race" lens for analyzing matters of discrimination.[23] Its virtue is that the socio-political race perspective meaningfully preserves an individual's ability to assert a varied personal identity, while providing a more effective tool for analyzing and addressing racism and pursuing equality.

The socio-political race concept of race views racial categories as neither a biological nor a cultural construction but rather as a group-based social status informed by historical and current hierarchies and privileges. This understanding of race diverges from some aspects of the literature on the social construction of race. Specifically, it jettisons the emphasis on personal identity in favor of a focus on the societal and political factors that structure opportunity by privileging and penalizing particular phenotypes and familial connections viewed as raced across groups. A socio-political race inquiry into the existence of discrimination does not examine a claimant's individual racial identity in a vacuum but rather the context of how the claimant was treated within any existing racial hierarchies.

For some, much about the socio-political race approach may just seem like a commonsense consideration of structural racism. Yet within the contemporary climate in which the social construction of race is misconstrued to mean the irrelevance of race, there is a newfound need for specificity and transparency in the articulation of the way continuing racialization of individuals is salient to the manner in which systemic discrimination occurs.[24] Without that specificity and transparency, the public impulse is to treat discrimination as a dynamic caused by the deviance of individuals unconnected to group-based hierarchies and structures of exclusion. Operating without the socio-political race approach has led multiracial-identity scholars to reduce inequality to a concern with the judicial and public recognition of personal racial identity that overlooks the issues of material inequality that are actually being raised in legal cases of discrimination.

While no single scholar has specifically lobbied for a socio-political race analytical lens per se, many have used other terms to address similar concerns that are relevant to the socio-political race analytical lens. For instance, the socio-political race concept combines Neil Gotanda's insights about the salience of remaining cognizant of past and continuing forms of racial subordination while appreciating how race can act as an indicator of social status.[25] The socio-political race perspective thus eschews both biological and cultural notions of race. W. E. B. Du Bois could be characterized as deploying a socio-political perspective on race regarding blacks in the United States when he famously stated, "But what is this group; and how do you differentiate it; and how can you call it 'black' when you admit it is not black? . . . I recognize it quite easily and with full legal sanction; the black man is a person who must ride 'Jim Crow' in Georgia."[26] For Du Bois, societal racial classifications were not based on innate self-identity but instead rooted in the forces of the socio-political subordination of his time.[27]

The abolition of formal Jim Crow state-mandated segregation has not lessened the significance of the socio-political race perspective for blacks, nor mitigated its application to persons without African ancestry. In her examination of Latino census politics, contemporary sociologist Nancy López uses the term "street race" in ways that resonate with the socio-political perspective.[28] López uses the term to describe the need for data collection forms to encourage respondents to consider how race data is used for monitoring social inequalities in ways that call for a response based on how others perceive one's race rather than how one personally identifies. Legal scholars Lani Guinier and Gerald Torres also implicitly deploy a socio-political view of race in their call for mobilizing people across racial categories to confront structural injustice as a matter of what they call "political race."[29] Guinier and Torres's "political race" encourages all races and ethnicities to draw upon the African American racial identity rooted in solidarity and focus on systemic problems.

What this book's socio-political race perspective particularly directs attention to are the ways in which even in the contemporary setting, racial differences are created and maintained for the social imposition of inferiority. The socio-political race perspective incorporates the sociological understanding that individuals are not born with a race. It is society that racializes an individual. Racialization then is a "systemic accentuation of certain physical attributes to allocate persons to races that are projected as real and thereby become the basis for analyzing all social relations."[30] Or as legal scholar Ian Haney López states, "[R]ace is not hereditary; our parents do not impart to us our race. Instead society attaches specific significance to our ancestry."[31] Sociologists Omi and Winant elaborate further on racialization as a racial formation that is a "sociohistorical process by which racial categories are created, inhabited, transformed, and destroyed."[32] Eduardo Bonilla-Silva helpfully refines the concept further with his idea of "racialized social systems" whereby societies structure economic, political, social, and ideological levels by the placement of actors in racial categories or races.[33] Each of these sociological explications of race as a racialization process informed by structural systems itself undergirds this book's socio-political approach to analysis of discrimination issues.

Applied to the context of multiracial discrimination claims, the socio-political race lens assesses whether a public duty bearer has racialized an individual as part of a mechanism for adverse treatment. A claimant's desire for public recognition of a personal multiracial identity standing alone will not suffice to make a legal claim of discrimination if the multiracial identity is not subject to being penalized. While a multiracial-identified person may feel slighted by any resistance to or questioning of his or her personal racial identity, such a slight is not tantamount to being denied access to employment, housing, public accommodation, or educational advancement on the basis of race.

Interestingly enough, none of the multiracial-discrimination-case claimants discussed in this book personally raised the concern with having their mixed-race identity recognized. In contrast, it has been the multiracial-identity scholars assessing the cases that have set forth this concern from the top down. Ethnic studies scholar Caroline Streeter has similarly noted that "[c]ompared with much of the academic writing by scholars of multiraciality, writing and video work by racially mixed women [is] far less invested in 'the right to choose identity' [and these women instead] align themselves with people of color [in their] strong critique of inequality and discrimination of all kinds."[34]

The voices of the multiracial claimants themselves suggest that the multiracial-identity scholars have misconstrued the nature of multiracial discrimination on the ground. Rather than presenting a unique form of discrimination, multiracial claimants are articulating a concern with being less favorably treated than those perceived as white. Even the small subset of cases in which African Americans are identified as the instigators of multiracial discrimination fail to impart a novel form of discrimination. Instead, the factual allegations follow the historical pattern of dark-skinned African Americans acting in a retaliatory fashion towards light-skinned persons they fear bear attitudes of superiority for how closely their skin or phenotype approximates whiteness (regardless of how far removed in ancestry the racial mixture is, as in the case of many persons of African ancestry who racially identify solely as black).

Perhaps it is not multiracial claimants themselves who are in need of the insights from the socio-political race lens for assessing discrimination claims, but rather the multiracial-identity scholars who contemplate their cases. In addition to assisting multiracial-identity scholars appreciate the reality of multiracial discrimination, the socio-political race lens may also assist them in more accurately assessing the salience of contemporary civil rights law. This book's survey of the cases themselves illustrates that contrary to the presumption of multiracial-identity scholars, judges do properly apply antidiscrimination law to multiracial claims even when they do not refer to claimants by their preferred mixed-race identity. Yet should future judges begin to exhibit confusion about how to analyze multiracial claims of discrimination, the socio-political race lens can be a useful analytical aid. Revisiting a case from a previous chapter will help to illustrate a useful application of the socio-political race lens.

For instance, in the 2010 employment case of *Nash v. Palm Beach County School District* (as discussed in chapter 2),[35] recall that Che Nash, a multiracial black and white teacher, brought an employment discrimination claim against his employer school district in Boca Raton, Florida.[36] In the court's search for mixed-race-specific animus (as promoted by multiracial-identity scholars) the court lost sight of the larger pattern of nonwhite workplace discrimination that may have affected the claimant. The court noted that the employer school did not dispute that Nash, "as an individual of mixed race, belongs to a protected class" and thus administered the claim on the basis of that status.[37] As a result, Nash's failure to provide credible evidence that similarly situated employees who were not mixed-race were treated more favorably, resulted in the dismissal of his case.[38] Inasmuch as mixed-race status is not necessarily apparent in a person's appearance, Nash and his employer may very well have had difficulty in identifying who in the workplace was multiracial. In the absence of evidence of specific mixed-race differentiation by the employer, there is a strong possibility that the court's strict adherence to Nash's request for a search for "multiracial" discrimination may have inadvertently undermined a fuller inquiry that could have detected a larger pattern of racial discrimination in the workplace that adversely affected Nash.

If Nash's lawyer had instead litigated Nash's experience within the socio-political race lens understanding of racism, his claim of discrimination would have been viewed as more persuasive. The most important litigation difference would have been for Nash's workplace displacement to have been directly situated as part and parcel of what other nonwhite teachers like himself were experiencing within the school district. Notably, the socio-political race perspective approach enables claimants to preserve their personal racial identity in describing themselves as multiracial while at the same time locating their experience as a racialized nonwhite person when that is applicable to their incident of discrimination. (The rare instances of allegations of discrimination at the hands of other nonwhites will also be aided by the socio-political race lens inquiry into how the particular context may esteem whiteness in the way the multiracial claimant was targeted. Chapter 2's discussion of dark-skinned-black color discrimination against light-skinned multiracial claimants in the workplace illustrates this.)

As applied to Nash, the socio-political race perspective would have highlighted the several instances in which Nash and the few African American teachers at the school were treated poorly in contrast to the white teachers (such as when Nash and the other nonwhite coaches were denied access to the practice facilities and training equipment provided to the white coaches). Explicitly harnessing the experiences of other nonwhites in the workplace as part of the nonwhite discrimination that he was also exposed to would have strengthened Nash's legal claim as a multiracial-identified claimant. This is the case because when the context of Nash's workplace is examined from the perspective of nonwhite versus white differentiation, rather than specific multiracial animus, a court is not limited to searching solely for evidence of how nonmultiracial persons were treated in comparison. Expanding the judicial inquiry into whether a broader pattern of nonwhite versus white differential treatment existed would have permitted the court to recognize how Nash was harmed by a workplace seemingly entrenched in a white over nonwhite hierarchy when he was dismissed from his coaching position and replaced by a white male with less seniority.

What this book's review of the emerging multiracial discrimination cases like Nash's reveals is the enduring operation of white privilege and the continuing societal problem with nonwhiteness in any form. Specifically, the cases illustrate the perspective that nonwhiteness taints rather than the concern that racial mixture itself is worrisome. Yet this insight is lost in the midst of the multiracial-identity scholars' singular focus on promoting mixed-race identity. Thus the socio-political race analytical lens is also meant to act as a corrective against the influence of such Personal Identity Equality platforms that have inclined the judiciary to discount the legitimacy of policies of inclusion like affirmative action on the basis of the presumed distinct racial position of multiracials.

Furthermore, the socio-political race analytical lens could be also a salutary intervention in the related dynamic of discounting the extent of discrimination that multiracials experience. For example, in the context of juror selection, some judges have allowed a prosecutor's alleged confusion about mixed-race prospective juror identity to justify rejecting that mixed-race person from jury service. While prosecutors can use their "peremptory strikes" to reject a prospective juror without any stated reason, federal and state constitutions prohibit prosecutors from rejecting prospective jurors from serving as jurors on the basis of their race. When prosecutors appear to be rejecting prospective jurors on the basis of their race, defendants can raise a *Batson* challenge and thereby inquire if there is a nondiscriminatory reason for striking the juror.[39]

The judge then must assess whether the prosecutor's proffered reason is merely pretextual and whether the defendant has shown purposeful discrimination.

When *Batson* challenges have been raised about rejecting mixed-race prospective jurors from jury service, some prosecutors have claimed that they were incapable of harboring discriminatory purpose in excusing the prospective juror because they were not even certain of the juror's race (while at the same time rejecting many other jurors of color).[40] A prosecutor's attempt to evade an inquiry into his or her discriminatory action by claiming confusion about a juror's racial identity is as a threshold matter problematic given the pervasive use of juror questionnaires that contain race and ethnic juror information, in addition to the ability to raise the question of juror racial identity during the *voir dire* questioning of prospective jurors.[41] More disturbing, though, is the reaction of some judges who assert that "the demonstrated uncertainty as to her race makes it less likely that [a juror] was challenged because the prosecutor believed she was black."[42]

This is disturbing in view of the fact that mixed-race jurors are often excused along with other jurors of color in a seeming pattern of blanket exclusion. Prosecutors are thus permitted to racially lump together presumably "racially ambiguous" jurors with other jurors of color they view as undesirable for jury service, while at the same time deflecting judicial inquiry with a claim of ignorance about the specificity of a mixed-race juror's ancestry. In effect, the mixed-race juror can be racialized and excluded from jury service while with a sleight of hand the racialized intent is veiled behind a claim of racial ignorance. Personal Identity Equality, with its emphasis on the distinctiveness of racial ambiguity, is incapable of articulating how the strategic recognition of ambiguity harms mixed-race prospective jurors, let alone a monoracial-identified juror whose appearance is also considered racially ambiguous. In fact, prosecutors have made claims of nonrecognition of race with monoracial-identified jurors as well as with multiracial-identified jurors.[43]

Unlike the Personal Racial Identity Equality approach, the socio-political race analytical lens pierces through the duplicity of the simultaneous recognition and nonrecognition of race. Rather than permitting a prosecutor's claim of nonrecognition of race to be examined in isolation and thereby characterized as a "race neutral" justification for excluding a juror, the socio-political race lens would examine the context of the exclusion. For instance, the socio-political race lens would find it relevant and significant when a mixed-race prospective juror is excluded in a larger pattern of excluding nonwhite jurors.

Support for the socio-political race analytical shift to examining *Batson* challenges in terms of overarching nonwhite juror exclusion (rather than examining individual racial group exclusion in isolation) can be found in New York's legal recognition of *Batson* challenges based upon skin-color exclusion.[44] New York's court of appeals specifically stated that "[p]ersons with similar skin tones are often perceived to be of a certain race and discriminated against as a result, even if they are of a different race and ethnicity. That is why color must be distinguished from race. . . . [D]ark skin color is a cognizable class and, indeed, must be one unless the established protections of *Batson* are to be eviscerated."[45] Similarly, the United States Second Circuit has clarified that distinct racial and ethnic groups may be combined for *Batson* purposes.[46] What the New York State Court of Appeals and the United States Second Circuit Court have recognized is that racial bias is often manifested in overarching nonwhite versus white terms rather than in the specifics of personal racial identity.

However, even in the absence of an entire pattern of nonwhite exclusion, the socio-political analytical lens would not treat a prosecutor's claim that he or she did not recognize a juror's race as race-neutral given the wealth of data demonstrating that human beings implicitly perceive racial and ethnic differences even when they do not acknowledge such recognition for themselves.[47] Moreover, a prosecutor's consciously subjective assessment of racial and ethnic identity is not salient to whether racial considerations are in play. For as one judge who has dissented from the treatment of prosecutor claims of nonrecognition of race as race-neutral has stated,

> There is no sensible method for reviewing, on a cold record, a prosecutor's subjective statement that he did not notice a prospective juror's race. . . . The whole point of *Batson* is that minority status can't be taken into account in jury selection when exercising peremptory challenges. A person with a minority heritage may bring valuable perspective to the factfinding process, and that is so whether or not the prospective juror "looks like" a minority to the prosecutor or trial judge.[48]

In other words, it is immaterial what a prosecutor's statements about perceived racial identity are when racial exclusion is the result. A more sound judicial approach to claims of nonrecognition of race is to acknowledge the existence of group-based social hierarchies and demand further justification for the juror rejection.

In short, multiracial victims of discrimination will be better served by legal analyses that seek to elucidate the continued operation of white supremacy when whites mistreat them because of their nonwhite status and when nonwhites mistreat them out of fear that light-skinned multiracial individuals will assert a racial privilege and impose a racial hierarchy. But this can only be done by shifting away from a focus on individual identity recognition to a focus on group-based racial realities. The socio-political race analytical lens is one path for doing so. For while "we do not choose our color, we [can] choose our commitments. We do not choose our parents, but we do choose our politics."[49] Importantly, we can choose social justice.

ACKNOWLEDGMENTS

I owe thanks to each person who generously read and commented on earlier versions of various book chapters: Taunya Lovell Banks, Paulette Caldwell, Devon Carbado, Tanya Coke, Jon Dubin, Mary Louise Fellows, Kevin Johnson, David Law, Robin Lenhardt, Jasmine Mitchell, Chinyere Osuji, Twila Perry, Deborah Post, Paul Secunda, Ian Weinstein, John Valery White, Patricia Williams, and the late Michael Zimmer. I was also greatly benefited by the opportunity to present chapters before the Harvard Law School Critical Race Theory Symposium, the Syracuse University Black Political Thought and Social Justice Workshop, the University of Pittsburgh Center on Race and Social Problems, the Fordham University School of Law Center on Race, Law & Justice Colloquium on Race and Ethnicity, and the Fordham University School of Law Faculty Scholarship Retreat. And last but never least are the Fordham University Law School librarians and the legion of research assistants who help me each and every day—thank you for all you do. Any shortcomings are entirely my own.

The following cases were briefly cited in the text as duplicating many of the same patterns presented by the primary cases discussed in the book as paradigmatic cases. This appendix provides additional details about those duplicative cases for interested readers.

Callicut v. Pepsi Bottling Group, Inc, No. CIV. 00–95DWFAJB, 2002 WL 992757 (D. Minn. May 13, 2002).

In *Callicut*, five claimants brought hostile work environment claims against Pepsi Bottling Group, Inc. (Pepsi). Although claimant Gentry McQuiston identified himself as biracial, the court called all the claimants African American, including McQuiston. Yet, as the following alleged facts detail, the racial harassment McQuiston described was about animus against his "blackness" and how white employees were esteemed in the workplace.

In 1999, McQuiston worked for less than a year as a temporary employee loading products onto trucks in Pepsi's Burnsville, Minnesota, warehouse. McQuiston asserted that while he worked with a racially diverse crew, many of the other work crews were racially segregated, with white employees being more favorably treated. McQuiston also described white coworkers being disrespectful to him with their barrage of racially charged commentary. For example, rather than referring to McQuiston by his name, a white coworker insisted on referring to him with racially coded nicknames such as "Sinbad," who is a black comedian, and "FUBU," which is an African American clothing line. After McQuiston informed human resources about these comments, the offending coworker was reprimanded and the name calling stopped. Furthermore, when McQuiston reported that a coworker had harmed him by stating that "he was not black," the coworker was suspended.

The court held that although it "did not doubt the sincerity of McQuiston's subjective beliefs," the instances of discrimination McQuiston alleged were not objectively sufficient to meet the established legal standard of "severe or pervasive" harassment that alters the conditions of employment. Therefore, the court dismissed McQuiston's claim. Importantly, the court's decision was firmly supported by the employer's documented response, which was to address each instance of alleged racial harassment as it arose rather than have it persist. As a legal matter, an employer can only be held liable for the racial harassment among coworkers if the employer was negligent in controlling the work conditions and in responding to the internal complaints of harassment. McQuiston's employer was quick to reprimand and suspend coworkers McQuiston found to be problematic. Thus McQuiston's lack of success was not caused by a judicial inability to understand the nature of multiracial discrimination but by the employer's actions in responding appropriately to the incidents in the workplace as they arose.

Khadaroo v. N.Y. Presbyterian Hosp, No. 10 Civ. 1237(CM)(RLE), 2012 WL 893180 (S.D.N.Y. Mar. 15, 2012).
Multiracial claims of discrimination are also treated as credible even when the claimants do not ultimately prevail. In the 2012 case of Camla Khadaroo, a complainant "of mixed-race background, which includes Black," brought a discrimination claim after she was fired for the third time from her position as a patient financial advisor at New York Presbyterian Hospital in New York City. The court stated that Khadaroo's "mixed race background qualifies as a protected class" and thus sought evidence of discrimination based on her mixed-race status. However, the court found that there could be no inference of race discrimination because Khadaroo admitted that race did not influence her last termination and the other two times she was fired did not fall within the time restrictions for filing a claim. Khadaroo's mixed-race identity was not a

barrier to proper judicial assessment of the claim despite its dismissal for procedural reasons.

Me. Human Rights Comm'n v. Coffee Couple LLC, No. 1:10-cv-00180-JAW, 2011 WL 2312572 (D. Me. June 8, 2011).

This successful lawsuit was filed in 2011 by the Maine Human Rights Commission on behalf of biracial complainant Anthony Verville and other coworkers. Verville identified himself as a "mixed race individual, both Caucasian and African American." His employer (the owner of a Tim Hortons coffee shop franchise) referred to him as "white nigger" and discharged him after Verville threatened to report him to the authorities for illegal payroll practices that unfairly reduced Verville's weekly wages. When the employer failed to continue defending himself in the lawsuit, the court entered a default judgment that awarded Verville lost wages and compensatory damages for the discrimination he experienced. The court did not raise a concern that Verville's biracial status should preclude his ability to raise a discrimination claim or pose particular evidence challenges. Indeed, the court characterized Verville as "a mixed race individual, both Caucasian and African American," and found that the employer's statements like "white nigger," among others, "arose from discriminatory racial animus."

Tabor v. Freightliner of Cleveland, LLC, No. 1:08CV34, 2009 WL 1175329 (M.D.N.C. May 1, 2009).

Another case in which the complainant alleged that his biracial status motivated the discrimination he experienced and the court "assume[d] without deciding" that complainant belonged to a protected class is the 2009 case of *Tabor v. Freightliner of Cleveland, LLC.* The complainant, Odis Tabor, a biracial black and white factory worker and union representative in Cleveland, North Carolina, claimed that he was fired because he is biracial. The former employer claimed he was terminated because "Tabor was a danger to [the] workplace"—a claim based upon two incidents when he threatened a coworker with physical violence. Tabor disputed the employer's justification and described ten incidents involving threats and assaults perpetrated by both black and white coworkers, who were not terminated as he had been. Nevertheless, the court found that Tabor did not provide adequate admissible evidence that those employees "engaged in comparable conduct and received less severe discipline for that conduct." Therefore, the case was dismissed on the basis of orthodox evidentiary concerns unrelated to Tabor's racial identity. The *Tabor* case thus serves as another example of a court having no difficulty applying the relevant antidiscrimination law with respect to a multiracial claimant.

Weatherly v. Alabama State, No. 2:10CV192-WHA, 2011 WL 6140917 (M.D. Ala. Dec. 8, 2011), *aff'd*, 728 F.3d 1263 (11th Cir. 2013).
This is an additional example of a multiracial colorism lawsuit success, in which a biracial woman alleged that her black female supervisor racially harassed her by repeatedly referring to her as "white bitch," and she was able to have the case heard before a jury that imposed $376,509.65 in monetary damages (a rare victory for any discrimination claimant).

EDUCATION CASES
Brooks v. Skinner, 139 F. Supp. 3d 869 (S.D. Ohio 2015).
The Brooks family of Ripley, Ohio, sued the school district on behalf of their biracial black children, who had been racially harassed by their peers with the repeated racial epithet of "nigger." It should again be noted that as in so many of the other multiracial claimant cases considered in this book, the Brooks children identified themselves as biracial but proceeded to articulate events that all targeted their African ancestry alone rather than their mixed-race status. The court refused to dismiss the case and the parties successfully reached a full settlement agreement.

DT v. Somers Cent. School Dist., 588 F. Supp 2d 485, 489 (S.D.N.Y. 2008), *aff'd* sub nom. *DT v. Somers Cent. School Dist.*, 348 F. App'x 697 (2d Cir. 2009).
J.L. was a student who experienced anti-black-focused racial harassment in the white suburban enclave of Somers, New York (a town in north-

eastern Westchester County within a seventy-five-minute train commute to New York City). Starting in 2004, J.L. attended ninth and tenth grades at Somers Central High School, where another student called him "nigger" in social studies class while crumpling his homework. He also alleged that other students in the cafeteria told him that he was not being a "good nigger."

The Somers Central High School responded to each reported complaint. When J.L. was harassed in the social studies class, the teacher reprimanded the student directly. When J.L. reported the harassment in the cafeteria, the acting principal conducted an investigation into the incident by speaking to all school officials in the cafeteria. The investigation yielded no indication that any of the students used the word "nigger" as alleged.

Later that academic year, J.L. was suspended from school for stealing a computer mouse from the school library's computer lab. He was suspended a second time that semester for breaking into school lockers with bolt cutters and joining his friends in stealing cell phones, iPods, and calculators. J.L. alleged that his bad behavior resulted from the school's deliberate indifference to the racial harassment he experienced. But given the high school's direct response to the classroom incident and its prompt investigation of the cafeteria incident, along with the clear factual basis for the suspensions, the court had justification to conclude that the high school was not deliberately indifferent to the allegations of racial harassment.

Lance v. Betty Shabazz Int'l Charter Sch., 2014 WL 340092 (N.D. Illinois 2014).
When four-year-old biracial student Myko Lance was expelled from the Betty Shabazz International Charter School in Chicago on November 19, 2011, his claim was dismissed for failure to provide any factual support for the allegation that his expulsion was due to what the court acknowledged as his "biracial" (African American and Hispanic) identity. It appeared that Myko's expulsion might have

been the fallout from a workplace dispute that his father, who was a teacher at the school, had with his coworkers and Myko's kindergarten teacher. Nevertheless, because the Chicago school system is only mandated to provide public school education beginning at the age of five, Myko did not have a legal entitlement to attend the kindergarten class at the time of his expulsion, and thus his case was dismissed. The dismissal was not caused by any judicial confusion with multiracial identity.

McClaskey v. La Plata R-II School Dist., 364 F. Supp. 2d 1041 (E.D. Mo. 2005).

In the face of the doctrinal challenges of proving discrimination claims in court, some claimants choose to discontinue the litigation. S.M., a junior at a La Plata High School in Missouri, made the choice to withdraw her claim in 2005. S.M. identified herself in her complaint as biracial, of "Negro and Caucasian parentage and ancestry," and noted that the school district was overwhelmingly Caucasian, with non-Caucasians making up less than 1 percent of the total student population of the school district. While S.M.'s complaint never detailed the exact racial slurs that she was targeted with during the student racial harassment, her narrative is one that focuses on what she perceives as the school's white/nonwhite divide. "[I]n relation to and comparison with her caucasian [sic] co-students, Plaintiff [complainant] S.M. received harsher and more frequent discipline, different and unfair process and procedures in the resolution of her grievances, different opportunities in educational and social school related programs and activities. . . ." (Complaint at 14, *McClaskey v. La Plata R-II School Dist.*, 364 F. Supp. 2d 1041 (E.D. Mo. 2005) (No. 03CV66)).

In the absence of an actual trial with definitive findings, the veracity of S.M.'s allegations cannot be determined. But what cannot be denied is the clarity of S.M.'s sense of racial isolation at the school, rooted in her nonwhiteness rather than her personal biracial identity.

Moore v. Board of Educ. of City of Chicago, 300 F. Supp. 2d 641 (N.D. Illinois 2004).

Andre, a mixed-race student of black and white ancestry in Chicago, Illinois, experienced anti-black-focused racial harassment. In 2004, the court found that the school district's choice to simply switch Andre out of the classroom of a teacher who targeted him with racially harassing comments could not rise to the legal standard of deliberate indifference. Neither Andre's school district nor the court reviewing his claim was inattentive to his allegations of racial discrimination simply because he identified as mixed-race.

HOUSING CASES

HUD v. Harris, HUDALJ 07–08–0396–8 Complaint (E.D. Mo. filed Sept. 24, 2009).

A similar pattern of anti-black bias tied to the presence of a black/white biracial child was evident in a case out of Rolla, Missouri, in which the court redacted the names of all the claimants (some were domestic abuse survivors probably seeking confidentiality). One of the claimants (complainant) was a white single mother with a black/white biracial son living in the owner's forty-four-unit housing complex. Soon after the complainant moved into the apartment, the property manager advised her not to have black visitors to her apartment after dark, presumably because the white neighbors would be frightened. The property manager thus stated, "Don't have colored people over scaring Ms. ——." The property manager repeatedly made derogatory remarks about black males during complainant's tenancy, including using the term "nigger." In one instance, the property manager told the complainant that he did not understand why she or other tenants wanted to be "with niggers" when "none of them pay child support." In another instance of the property manager repeating his litany of why black men were worthless, he referred to complainant's biracial son as a "nigglet." From the context of the conversations the complainant felt the derogatory statements about black males were also directed at her biracial son.

Numerous other tenants and former tenants confirmed that the property manager used the racial epithet of "nigger" along with making derogatory comments about blacks on a regular basis. He also referred to other biracial children as "nigglets" and "brown babies." The final straw arrived when complainant had black relatives from out of town staying with her for the weekend and the property manager called several times to yell and complain about the presence of her guests. The complainant moved out of the apartment and filed a complaint with HUD due to the stressful environment created by the property manager's racial discrimination. HUD's investigation revealed that the property manager had a practice of turning away blacks by informing them that no rental applications were available or that there were no units available.

The parties settled the case and complainant received twenty-five thousand dollars in damages (*U.S.A. v. Harris*, No. 09-CV-01859-CEJ Consent Decree (E.D. Missouri Nov. 20, 2011)). Moreover, the consent decree mandated that the property owner pay a thirty thousand dollar civil penalty to the U.S. government, in addition to the property manager himself having to directly pay a civil penalty of five thousand dollars. The consent decree also enjoined the property owner and his employees from any further discrimination, and mandated that they implement a nondiscrimination policy, attend fair housing training, keep records of rental applications, including race information, along with reporting on their records to the U.S. government every six months for a period of three years or longer should the consent decree's duration be extended further for noncompliance.

HUD v. Rogers, HUDALJ 08-08-0119-8 Complaint (D. So. Dak. filed Sept. 24, 2008).
Another case in which the participation of a nonprofit organization committed to the prevention and elimination of housing discrimination was instrumental in demonstrating the anti-black racism aimed at the black/white biracial relative of a white tenant occurred in Sioux Falls, South Dakota. Sioux Falls is also another predominantly white jurisdic-

tion where whites accounted for 86.8 percent of the 2010 census area population, while blacks accounted for 4.2 percent, American Indians 2.7 percent, Asians 1.8 percent, and persons selecting two or more races were 2.5 percent. When Starla Overbee moved into one of the sixteen apartment units managed by a marital couple in 2007, she advised them that she had a biracial (black/white) grandson who would be visiting her several times a week. After she resided in the apartment for two months, one owner told Starla that he did not rent to people with children or "Africans." Shortly thereafter, the second owner informed Starla that she had to evacuate the premises that same evening because her rent payment was overdue.

After Starla moved out, she contacted the Fair Housing of Dakotas organization for assistance. While the owners had never uttered a racial epithet regarding the racial ancestry of her grandson, Starla suspected that the owners' failure to follow the legally mandated rules for providing adequate advance notice to evict a tenant was motivated by some animus against her biracial grandchild. Standing alone, Starla's suspicions could not have been persuasive in court. However, the Fair Housing of the Dakotas (FHD) organization contacted several current and former tenants of the owners in order to discern if there were any patterns of racial discrimination.

The investigation uncovered that at least two current and former tenants indicated that the owners informed them that they did not rent to blacks. In addition, the FHD investigation of the owners' rental records demonstrated that the owners had never rented a unit to a black person prior to when Starla filed her HUD housing discrimination complaint. With the extensive evidence that FHD's investigation produced demonstrating how the discriminatory actions taken against Starla and her biracial grandson were anchored in the overarching anti-black bias the owners held, the owners agreed to settle the case.

The terms of the consent order mandated that the owners compensate Starla and FHD fifty thousand dollars in damages and attorney's fees, and pay a nine thousand dollar civil penalty to the U.S. government (*U.S.A. v. Phyllis Rogers*, No. 08–4175 Consent Order (D. S.D. Oct. 29, 2009)). Moreover, the owners were enjoined from any further discrimination, and mandated to implement a nondiscriminatory policy, undergo mandatory fair housing training, and maintain records of all rental applications, including racial data for reporting to the U.S. government on an annual basis for three years or longer should the consent order duration be extended for lack of compliance.

Krieman v. Crystal Lake Apartments, 2006 WL 1519320 (N.D. Illinois 2006).
Even in a case where the claimants had effectively waived their rights and were time barred, the allegations demonstrate the overarching salience of nonwhite bias for multiracial claimants. The claimants were Bridget and Darlene Krieman, the white mother and grandmother, respectively, of Anthony Krieman (whose father is black). While the Kriemans resided at the Crystal Lake Apartments in Chicago, Illinois, the apartment manager made numerous derogatory comments about Anthony's race, including calling him "nigger" and "biracial boy." While the Kriemans did not ultimately prevail with their lawsuit, the judge at no time questioned the legitimacy of Anthony's right as a multiracial claimant to file the claim. The judge explicitly stated, "Plaintiffs [complainants] are members of a protected class," and that the derogatory comments about Anthony's race did raise an issue about the manager's discriminatory intent toward the claimants.

U.S.A. v. Big D Enterprises, Inc., 184 F.3d 924 (8th Cir. 1999).
The owners of a Fort Smith, Arkansas, apartment complex had an explicit policy of not renting to prospective black tenants. When Cynthia Williams, a white mother, sought to rent an apartment in 1994, she was told that one or more apartments were available. But when the landlord discovered that Cynthia had a biracial child, the landlord refused to accept her rental deposit and tender the apartment key. The landlord stated that she did not want a "black child" living there. When the case went to

trial, the jury found that the landlord had violated the Fair Housing Act and awarded Cynthia and two other prospective tenants one thousand dollars in compensatory damages and one hundred thousand dollars in punitive damages. When the landlord sought to appeal the high punitive damages award, the court of appeals explicitly stated that the award was justified because the landlord had directly engaged in the systematic and deliberate exclusion of an entire race of people.

> Such action exemplifies racism in its rawest form. Appellants' acts of intentional racial discrimination demonstrate that this society's goal of providing housing free of racial bias has yet to be achieved. Punitive damage awards help ensure that citizens who engage in such contempt-able [sic] behavior against other citizens receive society's full rebuke and condemnation. The punitive damage award in this case promotes such an outcome and reinforces the nation's commitment to protecting and preserving the civil rights of all.

Thus while the judge consistently referred to Cynthia's son by the personal identity term "biracial" that she preferred for him, the judge was also attuned to the ways in which the landlord's insistence at excluding her son despite the presence of his white mother and his own white ancestry was connected to our nation's history of societal anti-black bias. The biracial personal identity did not alter how Cynthia's son was perceived for purposes of racial exclusion in a town in which 3 percent of the population identified with two or more races on the 2000 census (in comparison to the 2.4 percent of the national population with a multiracial identity in 2000). Even with the statistical dominance of whites in Fort Smith, Arkansas, representing 77 percent of the population, Cynthia's own white status was not sufficient to counter the landlord's aversion to blackness in any amount. The landlord instead treated her son as if he were part of the 8.6 percent of the population that identified solely as black. The town's 80,268 population size was also made up of 4.7 percent Asian, 1.7 percent American Indian, and Latinos of any race constituted 8.8 percent.

U.S.A. v. Kelly, No. 5:10-cv-00186-DCB-JMR (S.D. Miss. Nov. 18, 2010). Ms. Breezie Penny was also able to use the law to vindicate her claims in the majority black city of Vicksburg, Mississippi. In 2007, Breezie, a white mother of a black/white biracial child, rented an apartment after speaking alone with the property manager. After Breezie moved into the apartment building, the property manager visited the apartment to have Breezie sign the lease and Breezie's daughter, M.E., was present. This was the first time that the property manager had ever seen M.E. That same day the property manager asked a white tenant of another unit to inform her if the tenant ever saw any black visitors to Breezie's apartment, so she could "get her out of these premises" along with her "black and white child."

The property manager also informed another tenant and prospective tenant about her interest in limiting the number of black tenants along with making statements that she did "not like renting to black people, because all they do is cause trouble, especially black men," and that she "is trying to weed out all the black tenants at Shamrock to make it a better place to live." Thereafter the property manager served Breezie with an eviction notice. After Breezie's attorney spoke with the property manager, she relented and allowed Breezie to stay in the apartment until the end of her lease period but would not renew the lease or allow Breezie to continue renting the apartment on a month-to-month basis as permitted by the lease.

After being forced to move out, Breezie filed a Fair Housing Complaint with HUD. HUD investigated and found reasonable cause to believe that discrimination had occurred and brought a claim against the property manager and the owner of the apartment building. The property manager and building owner elected to have the HUD charge heard in federal court. Thereafter the parties entered into a settlement agreement wherein Breezie and her daughter were paid $17,500 (*U.S.A. v. Kelly*, No. 5:10-cv-00186-DCB-JMR Consent Decree (S.D. Miss. Mar. 20, 2012). In addition, the property manager and the building owner were required to attend a fair housing training session approved by the government, along with any new employees performing their same duties of screening tenant applications. Under the terms of the consent decree, the court retained jurisdiction for the following two years with the authority to extend the time if necessary to further supervise any violation of the decree or housing law.

CRIMINAL JUSTICE CASES

Burress v. Perkins, No. 2:13-CV-01970, 2014 WL 12538965 (S.D.W. Va. Feb. 28, 2014), report and recommendation adopted, No. 2:13-CV-01970, 2014 WL 12543919 (S.D.W. Va. Mar. 20, 2014), *aff'd*, 579 F. App'x 217 (4th Cir. 2014).

In 2014, Duncan Lamar Burress filed an Eighth Amendment claim because he alleged physical injury at the hands of three well-known white supremacist inmates when the "Correctional Officers" of the Mount Olive Correctional Complex in West Virginia brought him into the recreation yard during a time in which the white supremacist inmate faction dominated the yard. Upon his entering the yard, three white supremacist inmates proceeded to beat upon Duncan, presumably for invading their sacred white space. The altercation lasted for approximately fifteen minutes before any of the COs present intervened.

While Duncan identified himself solely as "biracial" in his complaint, with no further specification about his racial ancestry, in his allegations he was adamant about how he viewed the COs as culpable for permitting "known Caucasian white supremacist[s] to be placed into a recreational position with inmates that they are highly probable to harm and kill, and/or otherwise cause inmates of a non-Caucasian ethnic background to be placed into a situation" that makes them vulnerable to harm. Thus, Duncan felt victimized for being viewed as nonwhite and not specifically because he was racially mixed. However, Duncan's claim was dismissed because he had no evidence that the COs knew or had reason to know that he would be in danger from attack by being brought into the recreation yard and that they then disregarded an excessive risk to inmate health or safety.

Gilman v. Manzo, No. 2:03-CV-00044 WGH RL, 2005 WL 941676 (S.D. Ind. Feb. 24, 2005).

James was an inmate of mixed-race Native American and Caucasian ancestry incarcerated at the Wabash Valley Correctional Facility in Indianapolis. When James and several other inmates he identified as "non-Caucasian" were terminated from their positions at the prison Wire Harness Shop, while Caucasian inmates were retained, James filed a claim of racial discrimination. Specifically, of the eight inmates who were terminated, only two were white, and the others who were terminated were black, Hispanic, and of mixed-race like James. James considered the white versus nonwhite treatment of the inmates discriminatory.

However, in order to succeed with a Fourteenth Amendment equal protection claim of racial discrimination, it is not sufficient to demonstrate statistical disparities in how different racial groups are treated. The claimant must first and foremost prove that a specific intent to discriminate existed on the part of the relevant decision maker. When James was terminated, the plant manager who made the decision did so on the basis of a technician report of inmate errors he was provided in which the inmates were identified solely by their operator number and not by name or race. Thus, when James and others were terminated, the plant manager did not know who they specifically were, let alone their races. For this reason the court concluded that there was no proof of an intent to discriminate. James's mixed-race identity had no bearing on the onerous demand that the intent to discriminate legal standard imposes on all claimants.

NOTES

Asterisks appear before page numbers in some of the endnotes according to the way in which Westlaw paginates the court decisions that have not been published by the court and are solely issued by Westlaw itself. They call it "star pagination," and it is recognized by legal scholars.

PREFACE

1 Senna, "Mulatto Millennium."
2 I have used pseudonyms for all the personal names referenced in this preface in order to protect the privacy of my family and friends.
3 Haslip-Viera ed., *Taino Revival.*
4 Hernández, *Racial Subordination in Latin America.*
5 Candelario, *Black behind the Ears.*
6 Hall and Whipple, "The Complexion Connection," 4.
7 Hernández, "'Too Black to Be Latino/a/.'"
8 Banks, "*Mestizaje* and the Mexican *Mestizo* Self."

CHAPTER 1. RACIAL MIXTURE AS A PRESUMED COMPLICATION IN ANTIDISCRIMINATION LAW

1 Sexton, *Amalgamation Schemes*, 35.
2 Complaint, Brown v. City of Hastings.
3 Federal Bureau of Investigation, "2015 Hate Crime Statistics."
4 Jones and Bullock, "The Two or More Races Population."
5 Pew Research Center, "Multiracial in America."
6 Morning, "New Faces, Old Faces," 41.
7 Squires, *Dispatches from the Color Line*, 20.
8 DaCosta, *Making Multiracials*, 171.
9 Streeter, "The Hazards of Visibility," 303.
10 Review of Federal Measurements of Race and Ethnicity, 171 (testimony of Carlos Fernández, President, Association of MultiEthnic Americans).
11 Douglass, "Multiracial People," A26.
12 Morganthau, "What Color Is Black?" 63, 65.
13 Switzer, "6 Things Charities Should Know"; Frey, *Diversity Explosion.*
14 Chen, "Unloving."

15 Desfor, "'Race,' 'Ethnicity,' and 'Culture' in Hawai'i," 225.

16 Velasquez-Manoff, "What Biracial People Know," Sunday Review 1.

17 Davison, "The Mixed-Race Experience"; Eisenstadt, "Fluid Identity Discrimination"; Fernandes, "Antidiscrimination Law and the Multiracial Experience"; Leong, "Judicial Erasure of Mixed-Race Discrimination"; Rich, "Elective Race," 1533; Rives, "Multiracial Work."

18 Leong, "Judicial Erasure."

19 Fernandes, "Antidiscrimination Law and the Multiracial Experience"; Rives, "Multiracial Work," 1334.

20 Eisenstadt, "Fluid Identity Discrimination," 840–45.

21 Rich, "Elective Race," 1533.

22 Leong, "Judicial Erasure," 472, 511. It should be noted that Tina Fernandes and Scot Rives endorse the entirety of Leong's critique and only depart in how they think the legal system should respond.

23 *See, e.g.,* Callicutt v. Pepsi Bottling Group, Inc., at *1.

24 Jones and Bullock, "The Two or More Races Population"; Jones and Smith, "The Two or More Races Population."

25 Pew Research Center, "Multiracial in America."

26 Jones and Bullock, "The Two or More Races Population"; Jones and Smith, "The Two or More Races Population."

27 52 U.S.C.A. § 10301 (2017).

28 Longmire v. Wyser-Pratte.

29 U.S. Equal Employment Opportunity Commission, "Directive Transmittal: EEOC Compliance Manual."

30 U.S. Equal Employment Opportunity Commission, "Facts about Race/Color Discrimination."

31 U.S. Const. amend. XIV, § 1 ("nor Shall any state deprive any person of life, liberty or property, without due process of law; nor deny to any person within its jurisdiction the equal protection of the laws"). The Fifth Amendment similarly prohibits racial discrimination by federal government entities as well with its edict that "no person shall be deprived of life, liberty or property, without due process of law." U.S. Const. amend. V.

32 347 U.S. 483 (1954).

33 Title VI Civil Rights Act of 1964 (education as federally funded program); Title VII Civil Rights Act of 1964 (employment); Fair Housing Act of 1968.

34 McDonald v. Santa Fe Trail Transportation Co., at 278 (noting that civil rights statutes "are not limited to discrimination against members of any particular race").

35 Crenshaw, "Race, Reform, and Retrenchment," 1344 ("As expansive and restrictive views of antidiscrimination law reveal, there is simply no self-evident interpretation of civil rights inherent in the terms themselves").

36 Leong, "Judicial Erasure," 523.

37 Ibid., 528.
38 Ibid., 543.
39 Ibid., 549.
40 Eisenstadt, "Fluid Identity Discrimination," 841.
41 Piper, "Passing for White, Passing for Black," 30 ("[M]y public avowal of my racial identity [as Black although appearing White] almost invariably elicits all the stereotypically racist behavior that visibly black people always confront. . . .").
42 Onwuachi-Willig, *According to Our Hearts*, 207–64 (proposing that "interracial-ity" be added to the protected areas of coverage in antidiscrimination law statutes).
43 Fernandes, "Antidiscrimination Law and the Multiracial Experience," 197; Rives, "Multiracial Work," 1334.
44 Rives, "Multiracial Work," 1334.
45 Fernandes, "Antidiscrimination Law and the Multiracial Experience," 215.
46 Ibid., 197.
47 U.S. Equal Employment Opportunity Commission, "Uniform Intake Questionnaire" (question of race invites respondent to choose all categories that apply); U.S. Department of Education Office for Civil Rights, "OCR Discrimination Complaint Form" (open-ended question as to how discrimination was "based on race"); U.S. Department of Housing and Urban Development, "Form 903 Online Complaint" (open-ended question as to how housing was denied "because of your race").

CHAPTER 2. MULTIRACIAL EMPLOYMENT DISCRIMINATION

1 Román, "Looking at that Middle Ground," 330.
2 Mitchell v. Champs Sports.
3 Ibid.
4 Ibid. at 646–47.
5 Ibid. at 647.
6 Nielsen and Nelson, "Rights Realized?"; Berrey, Nelson, and Nielsen, *Rights on Trial*.
7 Clermont and Schwab, "Employment Discrimination Plaintiffs in Federal Court," 127.
8 Ibid.
9 *Mitchell* at 650.
10 Hernández, "One Path for 'Post-Racial' Employment Discrimination Cases," 307.
11 42 F. Supp. 2d 642, 645–47, 650.
12 Leong, "Judicial Erasure," 512–13.
13 Hernández, "Multiracial in the Workplace."
14 Martin v. Estero Fire Rescue; Jones v. HCA; De Markoff v. Superior Court of Cal; Motto v. Wal-Mart Stores East; You v. Longs Drugs Stores Cal.; Yegin v. BBVA Compass; Khadaroo v. N.Y. Presbyterian Hosp.; Weatherly v. Ala. State Univ;

Doyle v. Denver Dep't of Human Servs; Doner-Hendrick v. N.Y. Inst. of Tech; Richmond v. Gen. Nutrition Ctrs. Inc.; Maine Human Rights Comm'n v. Coffee Couple LLC; Graves v. Dist. of Columbia; Walker v. Univ. of Colo. Bd. of Regents; Nash v. Palm Beach Cnty. Sch. Dist; Marshall v. Mayor and Alderman of City of Savannah, Ga.; Marsden v. Arnett & Foster, P.L.L.C; Tabor v. Freightliner of Cleveland, LLC; Kendall v. Urban League of Flint; Smith v. CA, Inc.; Watkins v. Hospitality Group Management, Inc.; Callicutt v. Pepsi Bottling Group; Maury v. Ogle County, Il; Mitchell v. Champs Sports; Walker v. Univ. of Colo. Bd. of Regents, Civ. A. No. 90-M-932, 1994 WL 752651 (D. Colo. Mar. 30, 1994).

15 Marshall v. Mayor and Alderman of City of Savannah, Ga. (dismissing case for failure to first raise the claim with the Equal Employment Opportunity Commission of mixed-race female firefighter of African American, Hindu Indian, and Caucasian ancestry who alleged she was unfairly terminated for posting provocative pictures of herself at the fire station on her social media account when no other employees were terminated for similar offenses); Maury v. Ogle County, Il (dismissing untimely filed case of white woman allegedly denied employment when accused of "f——ing that nigger" when discovered she had a mixed-race child).

16 Leong, "Judicial Erasure"; Fernandes, "Antidiscrimination Law and the Multiracial Experience"; Rives, "Multiracial Work"; Eisenstadt, "Fluid Identity Discrimination."

17 Richmond v. General Nutrition Centers Inc.

18 Ibid.

19 Ibid.

20 Ibid.

21 Ibid.

22 Ibid.

23 Ibid.

24 Fed. R. Civ. Proc. 56.

25 Ibid. at *13, *16.

26 Hornby, "Summary Judgment without Illusions," 273, 279–80.

27 Martin v. Estero Fire Rescue (dismissing case because employer authorized to terminate claimant for violating workplace policy against illegal drug use); Jones v. HCA (dismissing the case because the claimant failed to notify the employer of the racial harassment and follow the employer's procedures for making a complaint as required by law before asserting employer negligence in not addressing harassment); De Markoff v. Superior Court of Cal. (dismissing case because employer selected a qualified white candidate instead of claimant without any demonstrated bias); Motto v. Wal-Mart Stores East (dismissing case because employer had the discretion to terminate claimant after violating the workplace policy against threats of violence); You v. Longs Drugs Stores (dismissing case because claimant failed to file the required initial administrative complaint with

the Equal Employment Opportunity Commission); Marsden v. Arnett & Foster, P.L.L.C. (dismissing the case because claimant was a non–U.S. citizen without authorization to work in the United States when he applied for the position); Callicut v. Pepsi Bottling Group, Inc. (concluding that the instances of discrimination alleged were not frequent or severe enough to meet the established legal standard of "severe or pervasive" harassment that alters the conditions of employment).
28 Smith v. CA, Inc.
29 Ibid. at *1,*11.
30 Ibid. at *11.
31 Burlington Industries v. Ellerth.
32 Beiner, *Gender Myths v. Working Realities*.
33 Leong, "Judicial Erasure," 518.
34 Ibid.
35 Stone, "Taking in Strays."
36 *Smith* at *1 n.1, *7.
37 Leong, "Judicial Erasure," 515.
38 Hernandez, "Latinos at Work."
39 *Smith* at *1 ("Smith claims [his supervisor] stated he was surprised an African American father like Smith would fight so hard for custody of his children.").
40 Leong, "Judicial Erasure," 517.
41 Maldonado, "Deadbeat or Deadbroke," 991, 994 (describing the societal bias against black fathers).
42 Watkins v. Hospitality Group Management, Inc.
43 *Watkins* at *3.
44 Banks, "Civil Trials."
45 Leong, "Judicial Erasure," 519.
46 Ibid. at 507.
47 Ibid.
48 Ibid.
49 You v. Longs Drugs Store (holding that complainant who described her race as "Hawaiian, Japanese, Korean, and possibly some Spanish" and who believes "others perceive her as 'mixed race, local'" and thus not as esteemed as her "Japanese-looking" coworker, was obligated to exhaust her administrative remedies before filing a federal discrimination claim).
50 Doner-Hendrick v. N.Y. Inst. of Tech.
51 Ibid. at *1, *6.
52 Ibid. at *1.
53 Ibid. at *1, *2, *6.
54 Ibid. at *6.
55 Ibid.
56 Ibid. at *2.

57 Ibid. at *6.
58 Stipulation of Dismissal, Dec. 12, 2012.
59 Goldberg, "Discrimination by Comparison."
60 Leong, "Judicial Erasure," 507.
61 Goldberg, "Discrimination by Comparison," 732, 754.
62 Doyle v. Denver Dep't of Human Servs.
63 Ibid. at *1, *18, *23.
64 Ibid. at *24.
65 Ibid.
66 Ibid. at *2.
67 Ibid. at *24.
68 Ibid. at *18.
69 Ibid.
70 Walker v. Univ. of Colo. Bd. of Regents, Civ. A. No. 90-M-932, 1994 WL 752651 (D. Colo. Mar. 30, 1994).
71 Ibid. at *1.
72 Ibid. at *1.
73 Walker v. Univ. of Colo. Bd. of Regents at *4.
74 Ibid.
75 Norwood ed., *Color Matters*.
76 Jones, "Shades of Brown," 1520.
77 Banks, "Colorism," 1733.
78 Walker v. Internal Revenue Service.
79 Banks, "Colorism," 1732–33.
80 Norwood, *Color Matters*, 35.
81 Harrison and Thomas, "The Hidden Prejudice in Selection."
82 Harrison, "Skin Tone."
83 Burch, "Skin Color and the Criminal Justice System."
84 Norwood, *Color Matters*, 29–31.
85 Hersch, "Profiling the New Immigrant Worker."
86 Goldsmith, Hamilton, and Darity, "Shades of Discrimination."
87 Hall, "The Bleaching Syndrome"; Hersch, "Skin Color, Physical Appearance, and Perceived Discriminatory Treatment"; Keith and Herring, "Skin Tone and Stratification."
88 Graves v. Dist. of Columbia.
89 Ibid. at 110, 112.
90 Ibid. at 112.
91 Ibid. at 113; Memorandum in Opposition to Motion for Summary Judgment Filed by Stephen H. Graves at 2, 4, Graves v. District of Columbia (hereinafter Graves, Memorandum in Opposition].
92 Graves, Memorandum in Opposition, 2, 5.
93 Ibid. at 3.

94 Ibid. at 4.
95 Ibid. at 16.
96 Ibid. at 3.
97 Ibid. at 13.
98 Ibid.
99 *Graves* at 113; Graves, Memorandum in Opposition, 6.
100 *Graves* at 123.
101 Issacharoff and Lowenstein, "Second Thoughts about Summary Judgment," 73, 89.
102 Weatherly v. Alabama State Univ. (awarding $376,509.65 in monetary damages).
103 Kendall v. Urban League of Flint.
104 Ibid. at 872.
105 Ibid. at 873.
106 Ibid. at 874.
107 Ibid.
108 Ibid. at 873, 884.
109 Ibid. at 873.
110 Ibid. at 881.
111 Ibid. at 881, 887.
112 Ibid. at 881.
113 Ibid. at 883.
114 *Kendall* at 888.
115 Yegin v. BBVA Compass. Arbitration disputes are resolved out of court by a neutral third party chosen to act as an arbitrator without the formalities and regulations of a court proceeding.
116 Banks, "Colorism."
117 Me. Human Rights Comm'n v. Coffee Couple (awarding lost wages and compensatory damages).
118 Nash v. Palm Beach Cnty. Sch. Dist.
119 Ibid. at *1, *5, *7.
120 Ibid. at *2.
121 Ibid.
122 Ibid. Excessing is a process whereby a school that has experienced a reduction in student population transfers some of its teachers to a school that needs them. Ibid. at *1.
123 Ibid. at *3.
124 Ibid. at *8.
125 Ibid. at *10.
126 Ibid.
127 Ibid. at *7.
128 Stone, "Taking in Strays," 149.
129 Oates v. Runyon (reinstating mixed-race black female U.S. Postal Service employee who was terminated for physical altercation with a female coworker

when manager took no disciplinary action against four white males for similar workplace misconduct); Brittany N. v. Fanning (dismissing claim of mixed-race human resources specialist in army who failed to rebut the army's non-race-based reasons for terminating his employment); Complainant v. McHugh (dismissing claim of brown-skinned mixed-race employee of an army contractor who was terminated by the contractor when the army found that sexual harassment charges lodged against the employee were substantiated and that it was the contractor who was responsible for his termination rather than the army); Lawson v. Donahoe (dismissing claim of mixed-race black employee who failed to rebut the employer's non-race-based reasons for suspending his training assignment); Rucker v. LaHood (2011) (dismissing claim of mixed-race black Federal Aviation Administration employee who failed to rebut the employer's non-race-based reasons for paging him back from a break and requiring a tabulation of sick days before authorizing additional sick leave); Rucker v. LaHood (2010) (dismissing claim of mixed-race black Federal Aviation Administration employee admonished for wearing boots that did not adhere to the agency dress code as he failed to identify a similarly situated employee who was more favorably treated when not complying with the dress code); Gonzales v. Potter (dismissing claim of mixed-race Mexican American of Native American and Caucasian ancestry against U.S. Postal Service employer for failure to allege personal loss or harm from specific change in term or condition of employment); Stethem v. Dalton (dismissing claim of American-Japanese mixed-race army employee who failed to timely raise his claim that his denial of a promotion was caused by the army preference to promote Caucasian males); Hill v. Runyon (dismissing claim of mixed-race U.S. Postal Service employee who failed to allege any harm or personal loss from a specific change in the conditions or terms of her employment from her manager's isolated remarks about her concern with discrimination); Lambert v. Brown (dismissing claim of Department of Veterans Affairs employee of Native American and Caucasian ancestry who failed to make timely complaint with the EEO/Equal Employment Opportunity counselor regarding allegation that he was passed over for a manager position in favor of less qualified employee); Ellis v. Runyon (dismissing claim of mixed-race African American U.S. Postal Service letter carrier who was terminated for being at fault in work-related motor vehicle accident and failing to identify how any other similarly situated employee was treated differently); Edgar, Loy v. USDA (dismissing claim of mixed-race Hispanic male forestry technician for U.S. Department of Agriculture because most of his coworkers were also of Hispanic and mixed heritage and had not been terminated).

CHAPTER 3. MULTIRACIAL DISCRIMINATION IN EDUCATION
1 Emma Brown, "Yale Study Suggests Racial Bias among Preschool Teachers," *Washington Post*, September 27, 2016. www.washingtonpost.com.

2 The one case excluded from this chapter's analysis is one in which the claimant failed to comply with the obligation to respond to her opponent's motion to dismiss, and the court was thus compelled to dismiss the case without a review of the merits. K.T. v. Natalia I.S.D (dismissing claim of mixed-heritage child of black and Mexican ethnicity alleging harassment based on her race and color).

3 Zeno v. Pine Plains Central School District.

4 Ibid. at 659, 663.

5 Ibid. at 659.

6 Ibid. at 660.

7 Ibid.

8 Ibid.

9 Ibid. at 662.

10 Ibid.

11 Ibid.

12 Ibid. at 659.

13 Ibid. at 662.

14 Ibid.

15 42 U.S.C. § 2000d (2017).

16 *Zeno* at 659.

17 Fulton v. Western Brown Local School Dist. Bd. of Educ., 2015 WL 3867243 (S.D. Ohio June 23, 2015).

18 Ibid. at *2.

19 Ibid. at *2.

20 Ibid. at *3.

21 Ibid. at *2.

22 Fulton v. Western Brown Local School Dist. Bd. of Educ., No. 1:15-cv-53 (S.D. Ohio Nov. 23, 2016) (court order of dismissal for settlement agreement).

23 Brooks v. Skinner (entering a settlement agreement).

24 DT v. Somers Cent. School Dist. (concluding school district not indifferent to student racial harassment because direct response to each incident alleged); Moore v. Board of Educ. of City of Chicago (concluding school district not indifferent to student racial harassment because direct response to each incident alleged).

25 Karlen v. Westport Bd. of Educ.

26 Ibid. at *2.

27 Ibid. at *2.

28 Lance v. Betty Shabazz Int'l Charter Sch (dismissing case of child under the age of five with no legal entitlement to attend kindergarten for children aged five and above).

29 Jackson v. Katy Independent School Dist.

30 Ibid. at 1301.

31 Smith v. Utah Valley University.

32 Barnett v. Baldwin County Board of Education.

33 McIntosh, "Unpacking the Invisible Knapsack," 33.

34 Flagg, *Was Blind, but Now I See.*

35 Graham v. Portland Public School Dist. at *2, *7.

36 Godby v. Montgomery County Bd. of Educ.

37 Ibid. at 1409.

38 Godby v. Montgomery County Bd. of Educ., Complaint par. 27.

39 Godby v. Montgomery County Bd. of Educ. at 1399.

40 Godby v. Montgomery County Bd. of Educ., Complaint par. 1.

41 Ibid. at pars. 33, 34.

42 Texeira, "The New Multiracialism," 32.

43 Cox, "What's Wrong with Biracial Label?" 2.

44 U.S. Department of Justice, "Justice Department Reaches Agreement with Alabama School District to End the Use of Race in Extracurricular Activities."

45 McClaskey v. La Plata R-II School Dist. (describing a black-white biracial student taunted with racial slurs in "an almost all-Caucasian school").

46 Shelton v. Mukwonago Area School Dist.

CHAPTER 4. MULTIRACIAL HOUSING AND PUBLIC ACCOMMODATIONS DISCRIMINATION

1 Ilyce Glink, "U.S. Housing Market Remains Deeply Segregated," Moneywatch. *CBS News.* June 20, 2012, www.cbsnews.com.

2 Larkin, "The Forty-Year 'First Step,'" 1617.

3 Meyer, *As Long as They Don't Move Next Door*, 197.

4 Otero v. N.Y. City Hous. Auth.

5 42 U.S.C. §§ 3604–05 (2017).

6 42 U.S.C. §§ 3612–14 (2017).

7 Southend Neighborhood Imp. Ass'n v. St. Clair Cty. (quotations omitted).

8 HUD ex rel. Jouhari v. Wilson.

9 Ibid. at *3.

10 Ibid. at *3.

11 Ibid. at *3.

12 Ibid. at *4.

13 Krieman v. Crystal Lake Apartments Ltd. P'ship (describing white mother of black biracial child called "nigger" by the apartment manager).

14 HUD ex rel. Bracken & Lin v. Fung.

15 Barkley, "Beyond the Beltway."

16 United States v. Big D Enterprises, Inc. (awarding a white mother of a black biracial child one thousand dollars in compensatory damages and one hundred thousand dollars in punitive damages for harm caused by landlord exclusion based on race); Compl., HUD v. Harris (awarding twenty-five thousand dollars in

damages to a white mother of a black biracial child racially harassed because of property manager's opposition to her "nigglet" son).

17 Krieman v. Crystal Lake Apartments Ltd. P'ship.

18 Cousins v. Bray, 297 F. Supp. 2d 1027 (S.D. Ohio 2003).

19 42 U.S.C. § 3604(a) (2017).

20 Cousins v. Bray, 137 F. App'x 755 (6th Cir. 2005).

21 Compl., HUD v. Richard Rogers et al. (noting the assistance of Fair Housing of the Dakotas organization in interviewing current and former tenants about the landlord's pattern of discrimination that affected the white complainant and her biracial grandchild).

22 Compl., HUD v. Beulah L. Stevens.

23 Ibid. at para. 12.

24 Ibid. at para. 13.

25 Ibid. at para. 14.

26 Ibid. at para. 14.

27 Consent Order, United States v. Beulah L. Stevens.

28 Kane v. Oak Trust & Sav. Bank.

29 Ibid. at *5.

30 HUD ex rel. White v. Kocerka (case misspells complainant Theresia White's name as Theresa).

31 Ibid. at *3.

32 Ibid. at *5.

33 Ibid. at *6.

34 United States v. Kelly & Cowart (awarding white mother of black biracial child $17,500 in damages because of anti-black racial harassment in white enclave building in majority black city of Vicksburg, Mississippi).

35 HUD ex rel. Alexander v. Tallent.

36 U.S. Census Bureau, "Pine Bluff, Arkansas."

37 Craig v. City of Yazoo City, Miss. (dismissing claim of white foster father of two biracial children who failed to offer any evidence that racism informed the zoning board's decision to enforce a zoning ordinance against him in prohibiting the installation of a portable building on his property).

38 Krieman v. Crystal Lake Apartments Ltd. P'ship.

39 United States v. Martin; United States v. Wilhelm; United States v. Witthar.

40 18 U.S.C. § 241 (2017).

41 McDonald v. Santa Fe Trail Transp. Co.

42 Jefferson v. City of Fremont, No. C-12-0926 EMC, 2012 WL 1534913 (N.D. Cal. Apr. 30, 2012).

43 Jefferson v. City of Fremont, 73 F. Supp. 3d 1133 (N.D. Cal. 2014).

44 Kilgore v. Providence Place Mall, No. CV 16-135 S, 2016 WL 3092990 (D.R.I. Apr. 1, 2016).

45 Kilgore v. Providence Place Mall, No. CV 16–135 S, 2016 WL 3093450 (D.R.I. June 1, 2016).

46 Brown v. Luxor Hotel & Casino, No. 2:14-CV-00991-MMD, 2014 WL 2858488 (D. Nev. June 23, 2014).

47 Brown v. Luxor Hotel & Casino, No. 2:14-CV-00991-RFB, 2015 WL 327748 (D. Nev. Jan. 24, 2015).

48 Brown v. Luxor Hotel & Casino, No. 2:14-cv-00991-RFB-GWF (D. Nevada July 20, 2016).

49 Robinson v. Erik Hicks, No. 1:07-CV-1751, 2010 WL 5697139 (M.D. Pa. Dec. 2, 2010).

50 Amended Compl. at 4, Robinson v. Erik Hicks, No. 07–1751 (M.D. Pa. Apr. 24, 2008).

51 Ibid. at *6.

52 Robinson v. Erik Hicks, 2010 WL 5697139, at *3 n.8 (M.D. Pa. 2010).

53 Ibid. at *3.

54 Ibid. at *8.

CHAPTER 5. MULTIRACIAL DISCRIMINATION IN THE CRIMINAL JUSTICE SYSTEM

1 George, "Invisibly Black."

2 Alexander, The New Jim Crow.

3 Russell, The Color of Crime; Eberhardt et al., "Seeing Black"; Harris, "Using Race or Ethnicity as a Factor."

4 Ross, "The Curious Case of Shaun King."

5 Patterson v. City of Akron.

6 Ibid. at 465.

7 Ibid. at 466.

8 Ibid. at 465.

9 Federal Rule of Evidence 801 generally prohibits the admission into evidence of a person's oral or written statement offered to prove the truth of the matter stated, when that person is not physically in court and able to be questioned.

10 Dormon ed., Creoles of Color.

11 Club Retro, LLC v. Hilton.

12 Ibid. at 193.

13 Ibid. at 213.

14 Ibid.

15 Ibid. at 202.

16 Capers, "Rethinking the Fourth Amendment"; Carbado, "(E)racing the Fourth Amendment."

17 Goodnough, "Harvard Professor Jailed."

18 Kowolonek v. Moore, No. 2008–154 (WOB), 2010 U.S. Dist. LEXIS 28716 (E.D. Ky. Mar. 25, 2010).

19 Ibid. at *2.

20 Kowolonek v. Moore, 463 F. App'x 531 (6th Cir. 2012).

21 Holliday, "Intonational Variation."

22 Antlfinger, "Three Ex-Cops Get Long Terms," B3; Gonzalez, "Voice of Calm and Reason Emerges"; "Marchers Want City to Take Note," B3; "Questions on the Blake Assault."

23 Johnson v. California.

24 Spiegel, "Prison Race Rights."

25 Villery v. Grannis, No. 1:10-CV-01022-RRB, 2013 WL 3340814 (E.D. Cal. July 2, 2013).

26 Villery v. Grannis, No. 1:10-CV-01022-RRB, 2013 WL 1499263 (E.D. Cal. Apr. 11, 2013).

27 Elise C. Boddie, "Racial Territoriality."

28 Burress v. Perkins, No. 2:13-CV-01970, 2014 WL 12538965 (S.D.W. Va. Feb. 28, 2014), report and recommendation adopted, No. 2:13-CV-01970, 2014 WL 12543919 (S.D.W. Va. Mar. 20, 2014), aff'd, 579 F. App'x 217 (4th Cir. 2014) (dismissing Eighth Amendment claim because biracial prisoner had no evidence that his correctional officers knew or had reason to know that he would be in danger from attack by being brought into the recreation yard during a time in which the white supremacist inmate faction dominated the yard).

29 Villery v. Grannis, No. 1:10-CV-01022-RRB, 2013 WL 3340814 (E.D. Cal. July 2, 2013), at *3.

30 Villery v. Grannis, No. 1:10-CV-01022-RRB, 2013 WL 4056260 (E.D. Cal. Aug. 12, 2013).

31 Byrum v. Tampkins.

32 Richard v. Fischer, 38 F. Supp. 3d 340, 355 (W.D.N.Y. 2014).

33 Ibid. at 355. A "five percenter" refers to a group called Allah's Five Percenters, which reflects the concept that 10 percent of the people in the world know the truth of existence, and those elites and agents opt to keep 85 percent of the world in ignorance and under their controlling thumb; the remaining 5 percent are those who know the truth and are determined to enlighten the rest. The Five Percenters was founded in 1964 in the Harlem section of the borough of Manhattan, New York City, by a former member of the Nation of Islam named Clarence 13X (born Clarence Edward Smith and later known as ALLAH the Father). Allah, In the Name of Allah.

34 Richard v. Fischer, 38 F. Supp. 3d 340, 347 (W.D.N.Y. 2014).

35 Association of State Correctional Administrators, "Aiming to Reduce Time-in-Cell."

36 Ibid., 352.

37 Richard v. Fischer, 2017 WL 3083916 (W.D.N.Y. July 20, 2017) (ordering correctional officers to comply with court-ordered discovery or risk court sanctions).

38 Lawrence, "The Id, the Ego, and Equal Protection." *See*, for example, Gilman v. Manzo, No. 2:03-CV-00044 WGH RL, 2005 WL 941676 (S.D. Ind. Feb. 24, 2005) (dismissing claim of mixed-race inmate who had no evidence of a specific intent to discriminate on the part of the prison officials who terminated him and several other nonwhite inmates from their employment in the prison wire harness shop).

39 Cannon v. Burkybile, No. 99 C 4623, 2002 WL 448988 (N.D. Ill. Mar. 22, 2002).

40 Cannon v. Burkybile, No. 99 C 4623, 2000 WL 1409852 (N.D. Ill. Sept. 25, 2000).

41 Ibid. at *5.

42 Leong, "Judicial Erasure," 518.

43 Cannon v. Burkybile, No. 99 C 4623, 2002 WL 448988 (N.D. Ill. Mar. 22, 2002), at *3.

44 Cannon v. Burkybile, No. 99 C 4623, 2000 WL 1409852 (N.D. Ill. Sept. 25, 2000), at *5.

45 Cannon v. Burkybile, No. 99 C 4623, 2002 WL 448988 (N.D. Ill. Mar. 22, 2002), at *1.

CHAPTER 6. PERSONAL RACIAL IDENTITY EQUALITY

1 Daniel, "Beyond Black and White," 334.

2 Walker, "Choosing to Be Multiracial in America," 68.

3 Moville et al., "Chameleon Changes," 514.

4 Ibid., 511.

5 Leong, "Judicial Erasure," 472, 511. It should be noted that all other multiracial-identity scholars endorse the entirety of Leong's critique and only depart in how they think the legal system should respond, as described in chapter 1.

6 *See, e.g.*, Callicutt v. Pepsi Bottling Group, Inc., at *1.

7 Leong, "Judicial Erasure."

8 Eisenstadt, "Fluid Identity Discrimination."

9 Rich, "Elective Race," 1569.

10 Fernandes, "Antidiscrimination Law and the Multiracial Experience," 213; Rives, "Multiracial Work," 1334.

11 Greene, "Categorically Black, White, or Wrong."

12 Joseph, *Transcending Blackness*, 24.

13 Daniel, *More Than Black?* 116.

14 Root, "Bill of Rights for Racially Mixed People."

15 Ibid.

16 Williams, "Linking the Civil Rights and Multiracial Movements," 88.

17 Joseph, *Transcending Blackness*, xvi.

18 Spickard, "Does Multiraciality Lighten?" 293.

19 Ibrahim, *Troubling the Family*, xxvi.

20 Johnston and Nodal, "Multiracial Micro Aggressions."

21 Gaskins, *What Are You?*

22 Dalmage, *Tripping on the Color Line*, 139.

23 Townsend and Berg Sicker, "My Choice, Your Categories."

24 Pinter et al., "It Matters How and When You Ask," 60, 64.

25 Root, "Factors Influencing the Variation in Racial and Ethnic Identity."

26 Curington, Lin, and Lundquist, "Positioning Multiraciality in Cyberspace"; Lee and Bean, "Reinventing the Color Line."

27 Lee and Bean, "Reinventing the Color Line."

28 Jackson, "Beyond Race."

29 DaCosta, *Making Multiracials*, 80.

30 Williams, *Mark One or More*, 111.

31 Williams, "Linking the Civil Rights and Multiracial Movements," 91.

32 Joseph, *Transcending Blackness*, xv.

33 Sexton, *Amalgamation Schemes*, 5.

34 Childs, "Multirace.com," 157.

35 Dalmage, *Tripping on the Color Line*, 171.

36 Lilla, "The End of Identity Liberalism" (critiquing the liberal obsession with diversity and the "omnipresent rhetoric of identity").

37 McCann and Kim eds., *Feminist Theory Reader*.

38 Currah, Juang, and Minter eds., *Transgender Rights*.

39 Ibid., 364.

40 Cross, "The Psychology of Nigrescence."

41 Demo and Hughes, "Socialization and Racial Identity among Black Americans," 372.

42 Worrell, "Nigrescence Attitudes in Adolescence, Emerging Adulthood, and Adulthood," 172.

43 Demo and Hughes, "Socialization and Racial Identity," 372.

44 Maddox, "The Cognition of Intersubjectivity."

45 Stewart, "Know Your Role."

46 Carbado and Gulati, *Acting White?*

47 Renn, "Creating and Re-Creating Race."

48 Cunningham "Colored Existence."

49 Oboler, *Ethnic Labels, Latino Lives*.

50 Portes and MacLeod, "What Shall I Call Myself?"

51 Min ed., *The Second Generation*.

52 Park, "Second-Generation Asian American Pan-Ethnic Identity."

53 Sexton, *Amalgamation Schemes*, 45.

54 Jones, "Mixed Race and Proud of It"; Gilanshah, "Multiracial Minorities," 183, 184.

55 Ibid., 186.

56 Ibid., 184.

57 See Transfer of Responsibility for Certain Statistical Standards from OMB to Commerce (hereinafter Directive No. 15).

58 44 U.S.C. § 3504 (2017).

59 Directive No. 15, at 19,269.

60 42 U.S.C. § 2000e (2017).

61 Ibid., § 3604.

62 Ibid., § 3605.

63 Review of Federal Measurements of Race and Ethnicity (hereinafter Multiracial Hearings), 267 (testimony of Paul Williams, General Deputy Assistant Secretary for Fair Housing and Equal Opportunity, U.S. Department of Housing and Urban Development).

64 52 U.S.C. § 10301 (2017).

65 Sexton, *Amalgamation Schemes*, 47.

66 Multiracial Hearings.

67 Office of Management and Budget, Hearing on Directive No. 15.

68 Revisions to the Standards for the Classification of Federal Data on Race and Ethnicity (hereinafter Revisions to Directive No. 15); Recommendations from the Interagency Committee for the Review of the Racial and Ethnic Standards to the Office of Management and Budget (hereinafter Recommendations to OMB).

69 Vobejda, "Census Expands Options," A11.

70 "OMB and Race."

71 "No to Multiracial."

72 Ga. Code Ann. § 50–18–135 (2017) (requiring a multiracial category on state forms used for reporting racial data to federal agencies); 105 Ill. Comp. Stat. Ann. 5/34–21.7 (2017) (requiring multiracial category on all forms used by the State Board of Education to collect and report on data that contain racial categories); Ind. Code Ann. § 5–15–5.1–6.5 (2017) (requiring a multiracial category in certain forms, questionnaires, and other documents used by public agencies); Mich. Comp. Laws Ann. § 37.2202a (2017) (requiring public agency forms and questionnaires that request racial information or classifications to include a multiracial category); Ohio Rev. Code Ann. § 3313.941 (2017) (requiring a multiracial category on school district forms that collect racial data); see also Stanley, "Census Bureau to Test Revised Race Categories," 1 (observing the administrative addition of a multiracial category to Florida's school enrollment forms and computers during a routine Department of Education update in 1995).

73 H.B. 2137, 50th Leg., 2d Reg. Sess. (Ariz. 2012) (proposing the addition of a multiracial category only to governmental forms that contain a survey relating to ethnicity); Md. Ann. Code art. 41, § 18–310 (1997) (repealed 2014) (authorizing a temporary task force to study the possible addition of a multiracial category on state forms); S. 252, 181st Gen. Ct., Reg. Sess. (Mass. 1997) (proposing the addition of a "multiracial" category on forms used by local school systems); H.B. 3796, 184th Gen. Ct., Reg. Sess. (Mass. 2005) (proposing the addition of a multiracial category on forms used by a federal agency that requires such information); H. 259, 1997 Reg. Sess. (N.H. 1997) (proposing mandatory inclusion of biracial and multiracial options on state forms that collect racial data); S. 1069, 74th Leg., Reg. Sess. (Tex. 1995) (proposing

mandatory inclusion of a multiracial category on state forms that collect racial data); H.B. 2031, 80th Reg. Sess. (Minn. 1997) (proposing that all state forms requesting information on racial identification include a multiracial category); S. 1439, 80th Reg. Sess. (Minn. 1997) (proposing that all state forms requesting information on racial identification include a multiracial category); A.B. 10560, 215th Gen. Assemb., 2d Reg. Sess. (N.Y. 1994) (proposing the addition of a multiracial category on forms produced and used by state agencies or schools); H.B. 2813, 69th Leg. Assemb. (Or. 1997) (proposing mandatory inclusion of multiracial category on certain forms requesting racial or ethnic identification); S. 545, 70th Leg. Assemb. (Or. 1999) (proposing mandatory inclusion of multiracial category on certain forms requesting racial or ethnic identification); H.B. 1537, 181st Gen. Assemb., Reg. Sess. (Pa. 1997) (proposing the addition of a multiracial category on certain government forms); H.B. 165, 2007 Leg., 69th Sess. (Vt. 2007) (proposing that forms used by state agencies that require a person to enter his or her race allow the person to indicate multiple races if appropriate or to indicate that the person is multiracial); A.B. 442, 92nd Leg., Reg. Sess. (Wis. 1995) (proposing the mandatory inclusion of multiracial category on forms by each state department and independent agency that requires racial or ethnic identification).

74 Atkins, "When Life Isn't Simply Black or White."
75 The Common Application.
76 Post, "The Salience of Race," 365.
77 Transcript of Oral Argument at 4, Grutter v. Bollinger.
78 Transcript of Oral Argument at 9–12, Gratz v. Bollinger.
79 Grutter v. Bollinger, 123 S. Ct. 2325, 2347 (2003).
80 Fisher v. Texas.
81 Transcript of Oral Argument at 32–34, Fisher v. University of Texas at Austin.
82 Fisher v. Texas II (Alito, J., dissenting).
83 Brief for the Am. Ctr. for Law as Amici Curiae Supporting Petitioner at *3.
84 Brief for Judicial Watch at *10.
85 Brief for Amicus Curiae of Pacific Legal Foundation at *18.
86 134 S. Ct. 1623 (2014).
87 A.R.S. Const. art. II, § 36; Cal Const., art. I, § 31; MCLS Const. art. I, § 26; OK Const. art. 2, § 36A; Ne. Const. art. I, § 30; Rev. Code Wash. (ARCW) (2017) § 49.60.400; N.H. Rev. Stat. Ann. § 21-I:52 (2017); Fla. Exec. Order No. 99–281 (Nov. 9, 1999).
88 "Colorado Discrimination and Preferential Treatment by Governments, Initiative 46."
89 Schuette v. Coalition to Defend Affirmative Action.
90 Schuette v. Coalition to Defend Affirmative Action (Scalia, J., concurring).
91 Ibid.
92 Davenport, "Beyond Black and White."

93 King, "Are African Americans Losing Their Footholds in Better Jobs?" 655; Smith and Welch, "Affirmative Action and Labor Markets," 280.

94 Clinton White House Staff, "Affirmative Action Review: Report to the President," *Almanac of Policy Issues* (1995), accessed July 27, 2016, www.policyalmanac.org.

95 Not all multiracials may agree that they are well served by programs of affirmative action. Multiracials of Asian and white ancestry, like applicants who solely identify as Asian or white, can presuppose that the civil rights objectives of affirmative action harm them by considering anything other than numerical test scores. However, this perspective overlooks the vast data that demonstrate that standardized tests are poor indicators of aptitude or assessing achievement. Allred, "Asian Americans and Affirmative Action." Standardized tests are primarily barometers of wealth status. Guinier, *The Tyranny of the Meritocracy*. When standardized tests are accurately understood as the proxy for wealth that they are, it is easier to comprehend how colleges presented with a multitude of applicants of all races with strong grades and achievements would devise a complex multifactor calculus for assessing the candidacy of each applicant. Stevens, *Creating a Class*. In a universe of many talented students with stellar high school records, no single candidate is necessarily more "deserving" than any other or guaranteed a "right" to be admitted. As one former admissions officer notes, "Contrary to what you might think, colleges do not want an entire school of A students with 1600s on their SATs. How boring!" Kramer and London, *The New Rules of College Admissions*, 124.

96 Blume and Long, "Changes in Levels of Affirmative Action in College Admissions."

97 Brown and Bell, "Demise of the Talented Tenth," 1261.

98 Saulny and Steinberg, "On College Forms, a Question of Race."

99 Brown, "Change in Racial and Ethnic Classifications Is Here."

100 Brown and Bell, "Demise of the Talented Tenth," 1248.

101 Massey et al., *The Source of the River*.

102 Brown, *Because of Our Success*, 151.

103 Sanchez and Bonam, "To Disclose or Not to Disclose Biracial Identity."

104 Good, Sanchez, and Chavez, "White Ancestry in Perceptions of Black/White Biracial Individuals."

105 Guinier, *Admissions Rituals as Political Acts*.

106 Leong, "Multiracial Identity," 15 (emphasis added). *See also* Deo, "Where Have All the Lovings Gone?" 411 n.11; Sekulow and Weber, "*Fisher v. University of Texas at Austin*," 94 n. 11.

107 Post, "The Salience of Race," 358.

108 Peery and Bodenhausen, "Black + White = Black."

109 Roth, "Racial Mismatch."

110 Brown and Bell, "Demise of the Talented Tenth," 1229.

111 Kirkland and Hansen, "'How Do I Bring Diversity?'"

CHAPTER 7. THE WAY FORWARD

1 Makalani, "A Biracial Identity or a New Race?" 107.

2 Walsh, "The Ideology of the Multiracial Movement," 220 (cautioning that "[u] nless the Multiracial Movement shifts its attention away from asserting the rights of individuals, however, its enduring legacy will be to sustain existing hierarchies").

3 Khaitan, *A Theory of Discrimination Law*.

4 Ibid., 2.

5 Lucas, "Undoing Race?" 1245.

6 Rich, "Elective Race," 1569.

7 Carbado and Gulati, "The Fifth Black Woman," 702.

8 Ibid., 717.

9 Rich, "Elective Race," 1505.

10 MacKinnon, "Substantive Equality," 10.

11 Ibid.

12 MacKinnon, *Butterfly Politics*, 464.

13 Ibid., 472–73.

14 Brown v. Board of Education.

15 MacKinnon, "Substantive Equality," 4.

16 Parents Involved in Community Schools v. Seattle School District No. 1.

17 Ibid., 2767.

18 Goodman, "Redacting Race in the Quest for Colorblind Justice."

19 Simon, Piché, and Gagnon eds., *Social Statistics and Ethnic Diversity*; Hernández, *Racial Subordination*.

20 Sexton, *Amalgamation Schemes*, 64.

21 Connerly and Gonzalez, "It's Time the Census Bureau Stops Dividing America."

22 Sexton, *Amalgamation Schemes*, 299.

23 Hernández, "'Multiracial' Discourse," 103.

24 Crenshaw, "Race, Reform, and Retrenchment," 1335.

25 Gotanda, "A Critique of 'Our Constitution Is Color-Blind,'" 4.

26 Du Bois, *Dusk of Dawn*, 153.

27 Appiah, *Lines of Descent*.

28 López, "Contextualizing Lived Race-Gender and the Racialized-Gendered Social Determinants of Health."

29 Guinier and Torres, *The Miner's Canary*.

30 Webster, *The Racialization of America*, 3.

31 López, "The Social Construction of Race," 38.

32 Omi and Winant, *Racial Formation in the United States*, 55–56.

33 Bonilla-Silva, "Rethinking Racism," 469.

34 Streeter, "The Hazards of Visibility," 313, 316.

35 No. 08–80970-CIV, 2010 WL 3220191 (S.D. Fla. Aug. 13, 2010).

36 Ibid. at *1, *5, *7.

37 Ibid. at *8.

38 Ibid. at *10.

39 Batson v. Kentucky.

40 People v. Inocencio.

41 National Jury Project Litigation Consulting, *Jurywork*.

42 Calhoun v. Yarborough.

43 People v. Barber.

44 People v. Bridgeforth.

45 Ibid. at 614–16.

46 Green v. Travis (quoting Powers v. Ohio, 499 U.S. 400. 416 (1991), "race prejudice stems from various causes and may manifest itself in different forms").

47 Banaji and Greenwald, *Blindspot*.

48 U.S. v. Guerrero (Circuit Judge Gould dissenting).

49 Lipsitz, *The Possessive Investment in Whiteness*, viii.

BIBLIOGRAPHY

STATUTES, CONSTITUTIONS, LEGISLATIVE MATERIALS, AND
GOVERNMENT DOCUMENTS

18 U.S.C. § 241 (2017).

42 U.S.C. § 1981 (2017).

42 U.S.C. § 1983 (2017).

42 U.S.C. § 2000d (2017).

42 U.S.C. § 2000e (2017).

42 U.S.C. §§ 3604–3605 (2017).

44 U.S.C. § 3504 (2017).

42 U.S.C.A. §§ 3612—3614 (2017).

52 U.S.C.A. § 10301 (2017).

105 Ill. Comp. Stat. Ann. 5/34–21.7 (West Supp. 1994).

A.B. 442, 92nd Leg., Reg. Sess. (Wis. 1995).

A.B. 10560, 215th Gen. Assemb., 2d Reg. Sess. (N.Y. 1994).

Arkansas Constitution art. II, § 36.

California Constitution, art. I, § 31.

Fair Housing Act of 1968, 42 U.S.C. § 3604 (2017).

Federal Bureau of Investigation: Criminal Justice Information Services Division. "2015 Hate Crime Statistics." United States Department of Justice, Federal Bureau of Investigation, Criminal Justice Information Services Division, 2015. Accessed January 24, 2017. www.ucr.fbi.gov.

Federal Rule Civil Procedure 56.

Federal Rule of Evidence 801.

Florida Executive Order No. 99–281 (Nov. 9, 1999).

Georgia Code Ann. § 50–18–135 (2017).

H. 259, 1997 Reg. Sess. (N.H. 1997).

H.B. 165, 2007 Leg., 69th Sess. (Vt. 2007).

H.B. 1537, 181st Gen. Assemb., Reg. Sess. (Pa. 1997).

H.B. 2031, 80th Reg. Sess. (Minn. 1997).

H.B. 2137, 50th Leg., 2d Reg. Sess. (Ariz. 2012).

H.B. 2813, 69th Leg. Assemb. (Or. 1997).

H.B. 3796, 184th Gen. Ct., Reg. Sess. (Mass. 2005).

Indiana Code Ann. § 5–15–5.1–6.5 (2017).

Maryland Ann. Code art. 41, § 18–310 (1997) (repealed 2014).

Michigan Comp. Laws Ann. § 37.2202a (2017).

Michigan Constitution art. I, § 26.

Office of Management and Budget, Hearing on Directive No. 15: Public Hearing on Standards for Classification of Federal Data on Race and Ethnicity (1994).

Ohio Rev. Code Ann. § 3313.941 (2017).

Oklahoma Constitution art. 2, § 36A.

Nebraska Constitution art. I, § 30.

New Hampshire Rev. Stat. Ann. § 21-I:52 (2017).

Recommendations from the Interagency Committee for the Review of the Racial and Ethnic Standards to the Office of Management and Budget concerning Changes to the Standards for the Classification of Federal Data on Race and Ethnicity. 62 Fed. Reg. 36,874, 36,885 (1997).

Review of Federal Measurements of Race and Ethnicity: Hearings before the Subcomm. on Census, Statistics, and Postal Personnel of the House Comm. on Post Office and Civil Service, 103d Cong. (1993).

Revised Code Wash. (ARCW) § 49.60.400 (2017).

Revisions to the Standards for the Classification of Federal Data on Race and Ethnicity. 62 Fed. Reg. 58,782, 58,788–90 (1997).

S. 252, 181st Gen. Ct., Reg. Sess. (Mass. 1997).

S. 545, 70th Leg. Assemb. (Or. 1999).

S. 1069, 74th Leg., Reg. Sess. (Tex. 1995).

S. 1439, 80th Reg. Sess. (Minn. 1997).

Title VI Civil Rights Act of 1964, 42 U.S.C. § 2000d (2017).

Title VII Civil Rights Act of 1964, 42 U.S.C. §2000e-2 (2017).

U.S. Census Bureau. "Pine Bluff City, Arkansas." U.S. Department of Commerce, Economics, and Statistics Administration, United States Census Bureau, 2010. Accessed September 29, 2016. www.census.gov.

U.S. Constitution.

U.S. Department of Education Office for Civil Rights. "OCR Discrimination Complaint Form." United States Department of Education, Office for Civil Rights, 2016. www.ed.gov.

U.S. Department of Housing and Urban Development. "Form 903 Online Complaint." Washington, D.C. www.portal.hud.gov.

U.S. Department of Justice. "Justice Department Reaches Agreement with Alabama School District to End the Use of Race in Extracurricular Activities." United States Department of Justice, Press Release No. 12-974, August 3, 2012. https://www.justice.gov.

U.S. Equal Employment Opportunity Commission. "Directives Transmittal: EEOC Compliance Manual." No. 915.003. The United States Equal Employment Opportunity Commission, Bloomberg BNA, and Bureau of National Affairs (Arlington, Va.). Washington, D.C.: Bureau of National Affairs, Section 15–7. Last modified April 19, 2006. www.eeoc.gov.

U.S. Equal Employment Opportunity Commission. "Facts about Race/Color Discrimination." EEOC. Accessed May 17, 2017. www1.eeoc.gov.

U.S. Equal Employment Opportunity Commission. "Uniform Intake Questionnaire." United States Government. www.egov.eeoc.gov.

CASE LAW

Barnett v. Baldwin County Board of Education. 60 F. Supp. 3d 1216, 1223 (S.D. Ala. 2014).

Batson v. Kentucky. 476 U.S. 79 (1986).

Brief for the Am. Ctr. for Law as Amici Curiae Supporting Petitioner at 3–4, Fisher v. Texas II, 136 S. Ct. 2198 (2016), (No. 14–981), 2015 WL 5317010.

Brief for Amicus Curiae of Pacific Legal Foundation, et al. as Amici Curiae Supporting Petitioner at 36, Fisher v. Texas II, 136 S. Ct. 2198 (2016), (No. 14–981), 2015 WL 5345847.

Brief for Judicial Watch, Inc., et al. as Amici Curiae Supporting Petitioner, Fisher v. Texas II, 136 S. Ct. 2198 (2016), (No. 14–981), 2015 WL 5345846.

Brittany N. v. Fanning. 2016 EEOPUB LEXIS 2875 (EEOC Oct. 28, 2016).

Brooks v. Skinner. 139 F. Supp. 3d 869 (S.D. Ohio 2015).

Brown v. Board of Education. 347 U.S. 483, 494 (1953).

Brown v. City of Hastings. No. 1:17-cv-00331 (W.D. Mich. Apr. 11, 2017).

Brown v. Luxor Hotel & Casino. 2014 WL 2858488 (D. Nev. June 23, 2014).

Brown v. Luxor Hotel & Casino. 2015 WL 327748 (D. Nev. Jan. 24, 2015).

Brown v. Luxor Hotel & Casino. No. 2:14-cv-00991-RFB-GWF (D. Nev. July 20, 2016).

Burlington Industries v. Ellerth. 524 U.S. 742, 765 (1998).

Burress v. Perkins. No. 2:13-cv-01970, 2014 WL 12538965 (S.D. W. Va. at Charleston Feb. 28, 2014).

Byrum v. Tampkins. No. ED CV 13–1843, 2015 WL 456723 (C.D. Cal. Feb. 2, 2015).

Calhoun v. Yarborough. No. CV 03–1962-DOC (JWJ), 2006 Dist. LEXIS 96214, at 17, 19 (C.D. Cal. Jan 30, 2006).

Callicutt v. Pepsi Bottling Grp., Inc. No. CIV. 00–95DWFAJB, 2002 WL 992757 (D. Minn. May 13, 2002).

Cannon v. CO Burkybile. No. 99C4623, 2000 WL 1409852 (N.D. Ill. Eastern Div. Sept. 25, 2000).

Cannon v. CO Burkybile. No. 99C4623, 2002 WL 448988 (N.D. Ill. Eastern Div. Mar. 22, 2002).

Club Retro, LLC v. Hilton. 568 F.3d 181 (5th Cir. 2009).

Complainant v. McHugh. 2014 EEOPUB LEXIS 274 (EEOC Jan. 30, 2014).

Craig v. City of Yazoo City, Miss. 984 F. Supp. 2d 616 (S.D. Miss. 2013).

Cousins v. Bray. 297 F. Supp. 2d 1027 (S.D. Ohio 2003).

Cousins v. Bray. 137 Fed. Appx. 755 (6th Cir. 2005).

De Markoff v. Superior Court of Cal. No. 1:11-CV-002017 AWI-MJS, 2013 WL 1896259 (E.D. Cal. May 6, 2013).

Doner-Hendrick v. N.Y. Inst. of Tech. No. 11 Civ. 121(SAS), 2011 WL 2652460 (S.D.N.Y. July 6, 2011).

Doyle v. Denver Dep't of Human Servs. No. 09-cv-03042-WYD-KMT, 2011 WL 5374750 (D. Colo. Nov. 8, 2011).

DT v. Somers Cent. School Dist. 588 F. Supp 2d 485, 489 (S.D.N.Y. 2008), *aff'd* sub nom. DT v. Somers Cent. School Dist. 348 F. App'x 697 (2d Cir. 2009).

Edgar, Loy v. USDA. 1987 EEOPUB LEXIS 2910, 87 FEOR (LRP) 22074 (EEOC Aug. 11, 1987).

Ellis v. Runyon. 1994 EEOPUB LEXIS 2696 (EEOC Mar. 1, 1994).

Fisher v. Texas. 133 S. Ct. 2411 (2013).

Fisher v. Texas II. 136 S. Ct. 2198, 2229 (2016).

Fulton v. Western Brown Local School Dist. Bd. of Educ. 2015 WL 3867243 (S.D. Ohio June 23, 2015).

Fulton v. Western Brown Local School Dist. Bd. of Educ. No. 1:15-cv-53 (S.D. Ohio Nov. 23, 2016).

Gilman v. Manzo. No. 2:03-CV-00044, 2005 WL 941676 (S.D. Ind. Feb. 24, 2005).

Gilman v. Manzo. No. 2:03-CV-00044, 2005 WL 4880622 (S.D. Ind. Sept. 6, 2005).

Godby v. Montgomery County Bd. of Educ. 996 F. Supp.1390 (M.D. Ala. 1998).

Godby v. Montgomery County Bd. of Educ. 996 F. Supp.1390 (M.D. Ala. 1998) Complaint.

Gonzales v. Potter. 2009 EEOPUB LEXIS 140 (EEOC Feb. 6, 2009).

Graham v. Portland Public School Dist. #1. 2015 WL 1010534 (D. Or. 2015).

Graves v. Dist. of Columbia. 777 F. Supp. 2d 109 (D.C. 2011).

Green v. Travis. 414 F.3d 288, 297 (2d Cir. 2005).

Grutter v. Bollinger. 123 S. Ct. 2325 (2003).

Hill v. Runyon. 1996 EEOPUB LEXIS 3187 (EEOC May 28, 1996).

HUD v. Beulah L. Stevens. HUDALJ No. 04–02–0703–8 Complaint (Ala. Apr. 4, 2005).

HUD v. Harris et al. HUDALJ 07–08–0396–8 Complaint (E.D. Mo. Sept. 24, 2009).

HUD v. on behalf of Angela Alexander v. Tallent. HUDALJ 06–96–1260–8, 1997 WL 718434 (Tx. Nov. 17, 1997).

HUD on behalf of Bonnie Jouhari and Pilar Horton v. Wilson and Alpha HQ. HUDALJ 03–98–0692–8, 2000 WL 988268 (Pa. July 19, 2000).

HUD on behalf of George White and Theresa White v. Kocerka. HUDALJ 05–94—0537–8, 1999 WL 290377 (Ill. May 4, 1999).

HUD on behalf of Meki Bracken & Diana Lin v. Fung. HUDALJ 07–053-FH, 2008 WL 366380 (Ill. Jan. 31, 2008).

HUD v. Richard Rogers, et al. HUDALJ 08–08–0119–8 Complaint (D. So. Dak. Sept. 24, 2008).

Jackson v. Katy Independent School Dist. 951 F. Supp. 1293 (S.D. Texas 1996).

Jefferson v. City of Fremont. 2012 WL 1534913 (N. D. Cal. 2012).

Jefferson v. City of Fremont. 73 F. Supp. 3d 1133 (N. D. Cal. 2014).

Johnson v. California. 543 U.S. 499 (2005).

Jones v. HCA. No. 3:13cv714, 2014 WL 1603739 (E.D. Va. Apr. 21, 2014).

Kane v. Oak Trust and Sav. Bank. 1995 WL 683820 (N.D. Ill. 1995).

Karlen v. Westport Bd. of Educ. 2010 WL 3925961 (D. Conn. Sept. 30, 2010), *aff'd* in part sub nom. Karlen v. Landon, 503 F. App'x 44 (2nd Cir. 2012).

Kendall v. Urban League of Flint. 612 F. Supp. 2d 871 (E.D. Mich. 2009).

Khadaroo v. N.Y. Presbyterian Hosp. No. 10 Civ. 1237(CM)(RLE), 2012 WL 893180 (S.D.N.Y. Mar. 15, 2012).

Kilgore v. Providence Place Mall. 2016 WL 3092990 (D. R.I. Apr. 1, 2016).

Kilgore v. Providence Place Mall. 2016 WL 3093450 (D. R.I. June 1, 2016).

Kowolonek v. Moore. No. 2008–154(WOB), 2010 U.S. Dist. LEXIS 28716 (E.D. Ky. Mar. 25, 2010).

Kowolonek v. Moore. 463 Fed. Appx. 531, 533 (6th Cir. 2012).

Krieman v. Crystal Lake Apartments. 2006 WL 1519320 (N.D. Ill. May 31, 2006).

K.T. v. Natalia I.S.D. 2010 WL 1484709 (W.D. Tex. Apr. 12, 2010).

Lambert v. Brown. 1994 EEOPUB LEXIS 4127 (EEOC July 8, 1994).

Lance v. Betty Shabazz Int'l Charter Sch. 2014 WL 340092 (N.D. Ill. Jan. 29, 2014).

Lawson v. Donahoe. 2013 EEOPUB LEXIS 2723 (EEOC Sept. 13, 2013).

Longmire v. Wyser-Pratte, 101 Fair Empl. Prac. Cas. (BNA) 1311, 90 Empl. Prac. Dec. P 42, 958 (S.D.N.Y. Sept. 6, 2007).

Maine Human Rights Comm'n v. Coffee Couple LLC. No. 1:10-cv-00180-JAW, 2011 WL 2312572 (D. Me. June 8, 2011).

Marsden v. Arnett & Foster, P.L.L.C. No. 2:07-cv-00678, 2009 WL 3644927 (S.D. W. Va. Oct. 28, 2009).

Marshall v. Mayor and Alderman of City of Savannah, Ga. 366 Fed. Appx. 91, 108 Fair Empl. Prac. Cas. (BNA) 1180 (11th Cir. Feb. 17, 2010).

Martin v. Estero Fire Rescue. No. 2:13-cv-393-FtM-29DNF, 2014 WL 3400974 (M.D. Fla. July 11, 2014).

Maury v. Ogle County, Ill. 2005 WL 78955 (N.D. Ill. Jan. 12, 2005).

McClaskey v. La Plata R-II School Dist. 364 F. Supp. 2d 1041 (E.D. Mo. 2005).

McClaskey v. La Plata R-II School Dist. 364 F. Supp. 2d 1041 (E.D. Mo. 2005) (No. 03CV66) Complaint at 14.

McDonald v. Santa Fe Trail Transportation Co. 427 U.S. 273 (1976).

Memorandum in Opposition to Motion for Summary Judgment Filed by Stephen H. Graves, Graves v. District of Columbia. 777 F. Supp. 2d 109 (D.C. 2011) (No. 1:07-cv-00156).

Mitchell v. Champs Sports. 42 F. Supp. 2d 642 (E.D. Tex. 1998).

Moore v. Board of Educ. of City of Chicago, 300 F. Supp. 2d 641 (N.D. Ill. 2004).

Motto v. Wal-Mart Stores East, LP. No. 11–2357, 2013 WL 1874953 (E.D. Pa. May 3, 2013).

Nash v. Palm Beach Cnty. Sch. Dist. No. 08–80970-CIV, 2010 WL 3220191 (S.D. Fla. Aug. 13, 2010).

Oates v. Runyon. 1997 EEOPUB LEXIS 785 (EEOC Mar. 13, 1997).

Otero v. N.Y.C. Hous. Auth. 484 F.2d 1122 (2d Cir. 1973).

Parents Involved in Community Schools v. Seattle School District. No. 1, 127 S. Ct. 2738 (2007).

Patterson v. City of Akron. 619 Fed. Appx. 462 (6th Cir. 2015).

People v. Barber. 200 Cal. App. 3d 378, 245 Cal Rptr 895 (5th Dist. 1988).

People v. Bridgeforth. No. 207, 2016 WL 7389277 (NYS Ct App. Dec. 22, 2016).

People v. Inocencio. No. A113380, 2007 WL 2783324 (Cal. Ct. App. Sept. 26, 2007).

Richard v. Fischer. 38 F.Supp.3d 340 (W.D.N.Y 2014).

Richard v. Fischer. 2017 WL 3083916 (W.D.N.Y. July 20, 2017).

Richmond v. Gen. Nutrition Ctrs. Inc. No. 08 Civ. 3577(LTS)(HBP), 2011 WL 2493527 (S.D.N.Y. June 22, 2011).

Robinson v. Hicks. No. 07–1751 (M.D. Pa. Apr. 24, 2008) Amended Complaint.

Robinson v. Hicks. 2010 WL 5697139 (M.D. Pa. Dec. 2, 2010).

Rucker v. LaHood. 2010 EEOPUB LEXIS 3246 (EEOC Sept. 17, 2010).

Rucker v. LaHood. 2011 EEOPUB LEXIS 406 (EEOC Feb. 18, 2011).

Schuette v. Coalition to Defend Affirmative Action. 134 S. Ct. 1623 (2014).

Shelton v. Mukwonago Area School Dist. 2009 WL 499323 (E.D. Wis. Feb. 27, 2009).

Smith v. CA, Inc. No. 8:07-cv-78-T-30TBM, 2008 WL 5427776 (M.D. Fla. Dec. 30, 2008).

Smith v. Utah Valley Univ. 97 F. Supp. 3d 998 (S.D. Ind. 2015).

Southend Neighborhood Imp. Ass'n v. St. Clair County. 743 F.2d 1207 (7th Cir. 1984).

Stethem v. Dalton. 2000 EEOPUB LEXIS 399 (EEOC Jan. 21, 2000).

Tabor v. Freightliner of Cleveland, LLC. No. 1:08CV34, 2009 WL 1175329 (M.D.N.C. May 1, 2009), aff'd, 388 F. App'x. 321 (4th Cir. 2010).

Transcript of Oral Argument, Fisher v. University of Texas at Austin. 133 S. Ct. 2411 (2013) (No. 11–345).

Transcript of Oral Argument, Gratz v. Bollinger. 123 S. Ct. 2411 (2003) (No. 02–516).

Transcript of Oral Argument, Grutter v. Bollinger. 123 S. Ct. 2325 (2003) (No. 02–241).

U.S.A. v. Beulah L. Stevens. No. 05–0295-KD-B Consent Order (S.D. Ala. Dec. 4, 2006).

U.S.A. v. Big D Enterprises Inc. 184 Fed. Rep. 3d 924 (8th Cir. 1999).

U.S.A. v. Guerrero. 595 F.3d 1059 (9th Cir. 2010).

U.S.A. v. Janie Kelly & Richard Cowart. No. 5:10-cv-00186-DCB-JMR (S.D. Miss. Filed Nov. 18, 2010).

U.S.A. v. Janie Kelly & Richard Cowart. No. 5:10-cv-00186-DCB-JMR, Consent Decree (S.D. Miss. Mar. 20, 2012).

U.S.A. v. Martin. No. 4:12-cr-00068 (W.D. Mo. Mar. 7, 2012).

U.S.A v. Phyllis Rogers et al. No. 08–4175 Consent Order (D. S.D. Oct. 29, 2009).

U.S.A v. Roger Harris, et al. No. 09-CV-01859-CEJ Consent Decree (E.D. Mo. Nov. 20, 2011).

U.S.A. v. Watford. 468 F.3d 891, 913 (6th Cir. 2006).

U.S.A. v. Wilhelm. No. 4:12-cr-00069 (W.D. Mo. Mar. 8, 2012).

U.S.A. v. Witthar. No. 4:11-cr-00205 (W.D. Mo. Aug. 31. 2011).

Villery v. Grannis. No. 1:10-cv-01022, 2013 WL 1499263 (E.D. Cal. Apr. 11, 2013).

Villery v. Grannis. No. 1:10-cv-01022, 2013 WL 3340814 (E.D. Cal. July 2, 2013).

Villery v. Grannis. No. 1:10-cv-01022, 2013 WL 4056260 (E.D. Cal. Aug. 12, 2013).

Walker v. Internal Revenue Service. 713 F. Supp. 403 (N.D. Ga. 1989).

Walker v. Univ. of Colo. Bd. of Regents. Civ. A. No. 90-M-932, 1994 WL 752651 (D. Colo. Mar. 30, 1994).

Walker v. Univ. of Colo. Bd. of Regents. No. 09-cv-01690-PAB-MEH, 2010 WL 5158377 (D. Colo. Sept. 27, 2010).

Watkins v. Hospitality Group Management, Inc. No. 1:02CV00897, 2003 WL 22937710 (M.D.N.C. Dec. 1, 2003).

Weatherly v. Ala. State Univ. No. 2:10CV192-WHA, 2011 WL 6140917 (M.D. Ala. Dec. 8, 2011), aff'd, 728 F.3d 1263 (11th Cir. 2013).

Yegin v. BBVA Compass. No. 2:12-cv-03882, 2013 WL 622565 (N.D. Ala. Feb. 19, 2013).

You v. Longs Drugs Stores Cal. LLC. 937 F. Supp.2d 1237 (D. Haw. Mar. 27, 2013).

Zeno v. Pine Plains Cent. School Dist. 702 F.3d 655 (2d Cir. 2012).

SECONDARY SOURCES

Affirmative Action Review: Report to the President, Clinton White House Staff. "Affirmative Action: Empirical Research." Chapter 3. Almanac of Policy Issues, 1995. Accessed July 27, 2016. www.policyalmanac.org.

Alexander, Michelle. The New Jim Crow: Mass Incarceration in the Age of Colorblindness. New York: New Press, 2012.

Allah, Wakeel. In the Name of Allah: A History of Clarence 13X and the Five Percenters. Atlanta, GA: A-Team Publishing, 2007.

Allred, Nancy Chung. "Asian Americans and Affirmative Action: From Yellow Peril to Model Minority and Back Again." Asian American Law Journal 14 (2007): 57–84.

Antlfinger, Carrie. "Three Ex-Cops Get Long Terms in 2004 Milwaukee Beating." Wisconsin State Journal, November 30, 2007. www.host.madison.com.

Appiah, Kwame Anthony. Lines of Descent: W. E. B. Du Bois and the Emergence of Identity. Cambridge, MA: Harvard University Press, 2014.

Association of State Correctional Administrators. "Aiming to Reduce Time-in-Cell: Reports from Correctional Systems on the Numbers of Prisoners in Restricted Housing and on the Potential of Policy Changes to Bring About Reforms." Association of State Correctional Administrators, Arthur Liman Public Interest Program, and Yale Law School, November 2016. Accessed June 18, 2017. www.law.yale.edu.

Atkins, Elizabeth. "When Life Isn't Simply Black or White." New York Times, June 5, 1991. Accessed June 12, 2017. www.nytimes.com.

Banaji, Mahzarin R., and Anthony G. Greenwald. Blindspot: Hidden Biases of Good People. New York: Delacorte, 2013.

Banks, Taunya Lovell. "Civil Trials: A Film Illusion?" Fordham Law Review 85 (2017): 1969–1985.

Banks, Taunya Lovell. "Colorism: A Darker Shade of Pale." *UCLA Law Review* 47 (2000): 1705–46, 1733.

Banks, Taunya Lovell. "*Mestizaje* and the Mexican *Mestizo* Self: *No Hay Sangre Negra, So There Is No Blackness.*" *Southern California Interdisciplinary Law Journal* 15 (2006): 199–233.

Barkley, Daniel W. "Beyond the Beltway: Compensatory and Punitive Damages in Fair Housing Cases." *Journal of Affordable Housing and Community Development Law* 7 (1998): 218–20.

Beiner, Theresa M. *Gender Myths v. Working Realities: Using Social Science to Reformulate Sexual Harassment Law.* New York: NYU Press, 2005.

Berrey, Ellen, Robert L. Nelson, and Laura Beth Nielsen. *Rights on Trial: How Workplace Discrimination Law Perpetuates Inequality.* Chicago: University of Chicago Press, 2017.

Blume, Grant H., and Mark C. Long. "Changes in Levels of Affirmative Action in College Admissions in Response to Statewide Bans and Judicial Rulings." *Educational Evaluation and Policy Analysis* 36 (2014): 228–52.

Boddie, Elise C. "Racial Territoriality." *UCLA Law Review* 58 (2010): 401–63.

Bonilla-Silva, Eduardo. "Rethinking Racism: Toward a Structural Interpretation." *American Sociological Review* 62 (1997): 465–80.

Brown, Kevin. *Because of Our Success: The Changing Racial and Ethnic Ancestry of Blacks on Affirmative Action.* Durham, NC: Carolina Academic Press, 2014.

Brown, Kevin. "Change in Racial and Ethnic Classifications Is Here: Proposal to Address Race and Ethnic Ancestry of Blacks for Affirmative Action Admissions Purposes." *Hamline Journal of Public Law and Policy* 31 (2009): 143–78.

Brown, Kevin, and Jeannine Bell. "Demise of the Talented Tenth: Affirmative Action and the Increasing Underrepresentation of Ascendant Blacks at Selective Higher Educational Institutions." *Ohio State Law Journal* 69 (2008): 1229–83.

Burch, Traci. "Skin Color and the Criminal Justice System: Beyond Black-White Disparities in Sentencing." *Journal of Empirical Legal Studies* 12 (2015): 395–420.

Candelario, Ginetta E. B. *Black behind the Ears: Dominican Racial Identity from Museums to Beauty Shops.* Durham, NC: Duke University Press, 2007.

Capers, I. Bennett. "Rethinking the Fourth Amendment: Race, Citizenship, and the Equality Principle." *Harvard Civil Rights–Civil Liberties Law Review* 46 (2011): 1–50.

Carbado, Devon W. "(E)racing the Fourth Amendment." *Michigan Law Review* 100 (2002): 946–1044.

Carbado, Devon W., and Mitu Gulati. *Acting White? Rethinking Race in "Post-Racial" America.* New York: Oxford University Press, 2013.

Carbado, Devon W., and Mitu Gulati. "The Fifth Black Woman." *Journal of Contemporary Legal Issues* 11 (2001): 701–29.

Chen, Jim. "Unloving." *Iowa Law Review* 80 (1994): 145–75.

Childs, Erica Chito. "Multirace.com: Multiracial Cyberspace." In *The Politics of Multi-racialism: Challenging Racial Thinking*, edited by Heather M. Dalmage, 157. Albany: State University of New York Press, 2004.

Clermont, Kevin M., and Stewart J. Schwab. "Employment Discrimination Plaintiffs in Federal Court: From Bad to Worse?" *Harvard Law and Policy Review* 3 (2009): 103–32.

"Colorado Discrimination and Preferential Treatment by Governments, Initiative 46 (2008)." *Ballotpedia*. Last modified September 3, 2013. www.ballotpedia.org.

The Common App. "The Common Application." Last modified 2017. www.commonapp.org.

Connerly, Ward, and Mike Gonzalez. "It's Time the Census Bureau Stops Dividing America." *Washington Post*, January 3, 2018.

Cox, Major. "What's Wrong with Biracial Label?" *Montgomery Advertiser*, November 6, 1996.

Crenshaw, Kimberlé Williams. "Race, Reform, and Retrenchment: Transformation and Legitimation in Antidiscrimination Law." *Harvard Law Review* 101 (1988): 1331–87.

Cross, William E., Jr. "The Psychology of Nigrescense: Revising the Cross Model." In *Handbook of Multicultural Counseling*, edited by Joseph G. Ponterotto et al., 93–122. Thousand Oaks, CA: Sage, 1995.

Cunningham, Julie L. "Colored Existence: Racial Identity Formation in Light-Skin Blacks," *Smith College Studies in Social Work* 67 (1997): 375–400.

Curington, Celeste Vaughan, Ken-Hou Lin, and Jennifer Hickes Lundquist. "Positioning Multiraciality in Cyberspace: Treatment of Multiracial Daters in an Online Dating Website." *American Sociological Review* 80 (2015): 764–88.

Currah, Paisley, Richard M. Juang, and Shannon Price Minter, eds. *Transgender Rights*. Minneapolis: University of Minnesota Press, 2006.

DaCosta, Kimberly McClain. *Making Multiracials: State, Family, and Market in the Redrawing of the Color Line*. Stanford, CA: Stanford University Press, 2007.

Dalmage, Heather M. *Tripping on the Color Line: Black-White Multiracial Families in a Racially Divided World*. New Brunswick, NJ: Rutgers University Press, 2000.

Daniel, G. Reginald. "Beyond Black and White: The New Multiracial Consciousness." In *Racially Mixed People in America*, edited by Maria P. P. Root, 333–41. Thousand Oaks, CA: Sage, 1992.

Daniel, G. Reginald. *More Than Black? Multiracial Identity and the New Racial Order*. Philadelphia: Temple University Press, 2002.

Davenport, Lauren D. "Beyond Black and White: Biracial Attitudes in Contemporary U.S. Politics." *American Political Science Review* 110 (2016): 52–64.

Davison, Ken Nakasu. "The Mixed-Race Experience: Treatment of Racially Miscategorized Individuals under Title VII." *Asian Law Journal* 12 (2005): 161–86.

Demo, David H., and Michael Hughes. "Socialization and Racial Identity among Black Americans." *Social Psychology Quarterly* 53 (1990): 364–74.

Deo, Shalini R. "Where Have All the Lovings Gone?: The Continuing Relevance of the Movement for a Multiracial Category and Racial Classification after Parents Involved in Community Schools v. Seattle School District No. 1." *Journal of Gender Race and Justice* 11, n. 11 (2008): 409–52.

Desfor, Laura Edles. "'Race,' 'Ethnicity,' and 'Culture' in Hawai'i: The Myth of the 'Model Minority' State." In *New Faces in a Changing America: Multiracial Identity in the 21st Century*, edited by Loretta I. Winters and Herman L. DeBose, 222–46. Thousand Oaks, CA: Sage, 2003.

Dormon, James H., ed. *Creoles of Color of the Gulf South.* Knoxville: University of Tennessee Press, 1996.

Douglass, Ramona E. "Multiracial People Must No Longer Be Invisible." *New York Times*, July 12, 1996. Accessed June 12, 2017. www.nytimes.com.

Du Bois, W. E. Burghardt. *Dusk of Dawn.* New Brunswick, NJ: Transaction, 1992.

Eberhardt, Jennifer L., et al. "Seeing Black: Race, Crime, and Visual Processing." *Journal of Personality and Social Psychology* 87 (2004): 876–93.

Eisenstadt, Leora F. "Fluid Identity Discrimination." *American Business Law Journal* 52 (2015): 789–857.

Fernandes, Tina. "Antidiscrimination Law and the Multiracial Experience: A Reply to Nancy Leong." *Hastings Race & Poverty Law Journal* 10 (2013): 191–217.

Flagg, Barbara J. *Was Blind, but Now I See: White Race Consciousness and the Law.* New York: NYU Press, 1997.

Frey, William. *Diversity Explosion: How New Racial Demographics Are Remaking America.* Washington, DC: Brookings Institution Press, 2014.

Gaskins, Pearl Faye. *What Are You? Voices of Mixed-Race Young People.* New York: Henry Holt, 1999.

George, Nelson. "Invisibly Black." *New York Times*, January 15, 2017. Book Review 14.

Gilanshah, Bijan. "Multiracial Minorities: Erasing the Color Line." *Law & Inequality Journal* 12 (1993): 183–204.

Goldberg, Suzanne. "Discrimination by Comparison." *Yale Law Journal* 120 (2011): 744–45.

Goldsmith, Arthur H., Darrick Hamilton, and William Darity Jr. "Shades of Discrimination: Skin Tone and Wages." *American Economic Review* 96 (2006): 242–45.

Gonzalez, Samuel. "Voice of Calm and Reason Emerges: Madison Police Shooting Not Just about Race because Victim Tony Tyrell Robinson Was Biracial, Says Family Spokesman Uncle Turin Carter." *Last Tradition*, March 10, 2015. www.thelasttradition.com.

Good, Jessica J., Diana T. Sanchez, and George F. Chavez. "White Ancestry in Perceptions of Black/White Biracial Individuals: Implications for Affirmative-Action Contexts." *Journal of Applied Social Psychology* 43 (2013): E276–86.

Goodman, Chris Chambers. "Redacting Race in the Quest for Colorblind Justice: How Racial Privacy Legislation Subverts Antidiscrimination Laws." *Marquette Law Review* 88 (2004): 299–364.

Goodnough, Abby. "Harvard Professor Jailed: Officer Is Accused of Bias." *New York Times*, July 20, 2009. Accessed June 12, 2017. www.nytimes.com.

Gotanda, Neil. "A Critique of 'Our Constitution Is Color-Blind.'" *Stanford Law Review* 44 (1991): 1–68.

Greene, D. Wendy. "Categorically Black, White, or Wrong: 'Misperception Discrimination' and the State of Title VII Protection." *University of Michigan Journal of Law Reform* 47 (2013): 87–166.

Guinier, Lani. "Admissions Rituals as Political Acts: Guardians at the Gates of Our Democratic Ideals." *Harvard Law Review* 117 (2003): 113–64.

Guinier, Lani. *The Tyranny of the Meritocracy: Democratizing Higher-Education in America.* Boston: Beacon, 2015.

Guinier, Lani, and Gerald Torres. *The Miner's Canary.* Cambridge, MA: Harvard University Press, 2002.

Hall, Ronald. "The Bleaching Syndrome: African Americans' Response to Cultural Domination vis-à-vis Skin Color." *Journal of Black Studies* 26 (1995): 172–84.

Hall, Ronald E., and Ellen E. Whipple, "The Complexion Connection: Ideal Light Skin as Vehicle of Adoption Process Discrimination vis-à-vis Social Work Practitioners." *Journal of Human Behavior in the Social Environment* (2017): 1–9. Accessed June 12, 2017. doi:10.1080/10911359.2017.1321511.

Harris, David A. "Using Race or Ethnicity as a Factor in Assessing the Reasonableness of Fourth Amendment Activity: Description, Yes: Prediction, No." *Mississippi Law Journal* 73 (2003): 423–70.

Harrison, Matthew. "Skin Tone More Important Than Educational Background for African Americans Seeking Jobs." *Multicultural Advantage.* Accessed June 6, 2017. www.multiculturaladvantage.com.

Harrison, Matthew S., and Kecia M. Thomas. "The Hidden Prejudice in Selection: A Research Investigation on Skin Color Bias." *Journal of Applied Social Psychology* 39 (2009): 134–68.

Haslip-Viera, Gabriel, ed. *Taino Revival: Critical Perspectives on Puerto Rican Identity and Cultural Politics.* Princeton, NJ: Markus Wiener, 2001.

Hernández, Tanya Katerí. "Latinos at Work: When Color Discrimination Involves More Than Color." In *Shades of Difference: Why Skin Color Matters*, edited by Nakano Glen, 237–41. Stanford, CA: Stanford University Press, 2009.

Hernández, Tanya Katerí. "'Multiracial' Discourse: Racial Classifications in an Era of Color-Blind Jurisprudence." *Maryland Law Review* 57 (1998): 97–173.

Hernández, Tanya Katerí. "Multiracial in the Workplace: A New Kind of Discrimination?" In *Gender, Race, and Ethnicity in the Workplace: Emerging Issues and Enduring Challenges*, edited by Margaret F. Karsten, 3–25. Santa Barbara, CA: Praeger ABC-CLIO, 2016.

Hernández, Tanya Katerí. "One Path for 'Post-Racial' Employment Discrimination Cases: The Implicit Association Test Research as Social Framework Evidence." *Journal of Law & Inequality* 32 (2014): 307–44.

Hernández, Tanya Katerí. *Racial Subordination in Latin America: The Role of the State, Customary Law, and the New Civil Rights Response*. New York: Cambridge University Press, 2013.

Hernández, Tanya Katerí. "'Too Black to Be Latino/a': Blackness and Blacks as Foreigners in Latino Studies." *Latino Studies* 1 (2013): 153–59.

Hersch, Joni. "Profiling the New Immigrant Worker: The Effect of Skin Color and Height." *Journal of Labor Economics* 26 (2008): 345–86.

Hersch, Joni. "Skin Color, Physical Appearance, and Perceived Discriminatory Treatment." *Journal of Socio-Economics* 40 (2011): 671–78.

Holliday, Nicole Reannon. "Intonational Variation, Linguistic Style, and the Black/Biracial Experience." PhD diss., New York University, 2016.

Hornby, Brock D. "Summary Judgment without Illusions." *Green Bag 2d* 13 (Spring 2010): 273–88.

Ibrahim, Habiba. *Troubling the Family: The Promise of Personhood and the Rise of Multiracialism*. Minneapolis: University of Minnesota Press, 2012.

Issacharoff, Samuel, and George Loewenstein. "Second Thoughts about Summary Judgment." *Yale Law Journal* 100 (1990): 73–126.

Jackson, K. F. "Beyond Race: Examining the Cultural Identity of Multiracial Individuals." PhD diss., State University of New York at Buffalo, 2007.

Johnston, Marc P., and Kevin L. Nodal. "Multiracial Micro Aggressions: Exposing Monocracies in Everyday Life and Clinical Practice." In *Micro Aggressions and Marginality: Manifestation, Dynamics, and Impact*, edited by Dread Wing Sue, 132–37. New York: Wiley, 2010.

Jones, Linda. "Mixed-Race and Proud of It." *Gannett News Service*, November 20, 1990.

Jones, Nicholas A., and Jungmiwha Bullock. "The Two or More Races Population: 2010 Census Briefs." U.S. Department of Commerce, Economics, and Statistics Administration, United States Census Bureau, 2012. www.census.gov.

Jones, Nicholas A., and Amy Symens Smith. "The Two or More Races Population: 2000 Census Brief." U.S. Department of Commerce, Economics, and Statistics Administration, United States Census Bureau, 2001. www.census.gov.

Jones, Trina. "Shades of Brown: The Law of Skin Color." *Duke Law Journal* 49 (2000): 1487–1557.

Joseph, Ralina L. *Transcending Blackness: From the New Millennium Mulatta to the Exceptional Multiracial*. Durham, NC: Duke University Press, 2013.

Keith, Verna M., and Cedric Herring. "Skin Tone and Stratification in the Black Community." *American Journal of Sociology* 97 (1991): 760–78.

Khaitan, Tarunabh. *A Theory of Discrimination Law*. New York: Oxford University Press, 2015.

King, Mary C. "Are African Americans Losing Their Footholds in Better Jobs?" *Journal of Economic Issues* 32 (1998): 655–68.

Kirkland, Anna, and Ben B. Hansen. "'How Do I Bring Diversity?' Race and Class in the College Admissions Essay." *Law & Society Review* 45 (2011): 103–38.

Kramer, Stephen, and Michael London. *The New Rules of College Admissions: Ten Former Admissions Officers Reveal What It Takes to Get into College Today*. New York: Fireside, 2006.

Larkin, Brian Patrick. "The Forty-Year 'First Step': The Fair Housing Act as an Incomplete Tool for Suburban Integration." *Columbia Law Review* 107 (2007): 1617–54.

Lawrence, Charles R., III. "The Id, the Ego, and Equal Protection: Reckoning with Unconscious Bias." *Stanford Law Review* 39 (1987): 317–88.

Lee, Jennifer, and Frank D. Bean. "Reinventing the Color Line: Immigration and America's New Racial/Ethnic Divide." *Social Forces* 86 (2007): 561–86.

Leong, Nancy. "Judicial Erasure of Mixed-Race Discrimination." *American University Law Review* 59 (2010): 469–555.

Leong, Nancy. "Multiracial Identity and Affirmative Action." *Asian Pacific American Law Journal* 12 (2006): 1–24.

Lilla, Mark. "The End of Identity Liberalism." *New York Times*, November 20, 2016. Accessed June 12, 2017. www.nytimes.com.

Lipsitz, George. *The Possessive Investment in Whiteness: How White People Profit from Identity Politics*. Philadelphia: Temple University Press, 1998.

López, Ian Haney. "The Social Construction of Race: Some Observations on Illusion, Fabrication, and Choice." *Harvard Civil Rights–Civil Liberties Law Review* 29 (1994): 1–38.

López, Nancy. "Contextualizing Lived Race-Gender and the Racialized-Gendered Social Determinants of Health." In *Mapping "Race": Critical Approaches to Health Disparities Research*, edited by Laura E. Gómez and Nancy López. New Brunswick, NJ: Rutgers University Press, 2013.

Lucas, Lauren Sudeall. "Undoing Race? Reconciling Multiracial Identity with Equal Protection." *California Law Review* 102 (2014): 1243–1452.

MacKinnon, Catharine A. *Butterfly Politics*. Cambridge, MA: Harvard University Press, 2017.

MacKinnon, Catharine A. "Substantive Equality: A Perspective." *Minnesota Law Review* 96 (2011): 1–27.

Maddox, Candace E. "The Cognition of Intersubjectivity: Neo Collective Narratives for Black Students at a Predominantly White Institution." PhD diss., University of Georgia, 2011.

Makalani, Minkah. "A Biracial Identity or a New Race?" *Souls* 3 (2001): 83–112.

Maldonado, Solangel. "Deadbeat or Deadbroke: Redefining Child Support for Poor Fathers." *U.C. Davis Law Review* 39 (2006): 991–1024.

"Marchers Want City to Take Note." *Indianapolis Star*, September 8, 2010.

Massey, Douglas S., et al. *The Source of the River: The Social Origins of Freshmen at America's Selective Colleges and Universities*. Princeton, NJ: Princeton University Press, 2003.

McCann, Carole, and Seung-kyung Kim, eds. *Feminist Theory Reader: Local and Global Perspectives*. 3rd ed. New York: Routledge, Taylor, and Francis Group, 2013.

McClain, Kimberly DaCosta. *Making Multiracials: State, Family, and Market in the Redrawing of the Color Line.* Stanford, CA: Stanford University Press, 2007.

McIntosh, Peggy. "Unpacking the Invisible Knapsack: White Privilege." *Creation Spirituality* (January–February 1992): 33–35.

Meyer, Stephen Grant. *As Long as They Don't Move Next Door: Segregation and Racial Conflict in American Neighborhoods.* Lanham, MD: Rowman & Littlefield, 2000.

Min, Pyong Gap, ed. *The Second Generation: Ethnic Identity among Asian Americans.* Walnut Creek, CA: AltaMira, 2002.

Morganthau, Tom. "What Color Is Black?" *Newsweek*, February 13, 1995. Accessed June 12, 2017. www.newsweek.com.

Morning, Ann. "New Faces, Old Faces: Counting the Multiracial Population Past and Present." In *New Faces in a Changing America: Multiracial Identity in the 21st Century*, edited by Loretta I. Winters and Herman L. DeBose, 41–67. Thousand Oaks, CA: Sage, 2003.

Moville, Marie L., et al. "Chameleon Changes: An Exploration of Racial Identity Themes of Multiracial People." *Journal of Counseling Psychology* 52 (2005): 507–16.

National Jury Project Litigation Consulting. *Jurywork: Systematic Techniques.* 2nd ed. § 5.45. Deerfield, IL: Clark Boardman Callaghan, 2016.

Nielsen, Laura Beth, and Robert L. Nelson. "Rights Realized? An Empirical Analysis of Employment Discrimination Litigation as a Claiming System." *Wisconsin Law Review* 2005 (2005): 663–711.

"No to Multiracial." In *All Things Considered.* National Public Radio broadcast. July 8, 1997. Also available in LEXIS, News Library, Tnpr File.

Norwood, Kimberly Jade, ed. *Color Matters: Skin Tone Bias and the Myth of a Post-Racial America.* New York: Routledge, 2014.

Oboler, Suzanne. *Ethnic Labels, Latino Lives: Identity and the Politics of (Re)Presentation in the United States.* Minneapolis: University of Minnesota Press, 1995.

"OMB and Race." In *All Things Considered.* National Public Radio broadcast. October 29, 1997. Also available in 1997 WL 12834140.

Omi, Michael, and Howard Winant. *Racial Formation in the United States: From the 1960s to the 1990s.* 2nd ed. New York: Routledge, 1994.

Onwuachi-Willig, Angela. *According to Our Hearts: Rhinelander v. Rhinelander and the Law of the Multiracial Family.* New Haven, CT: Yale University Press, 2013.

Park, Jerry Z. "Second-Generation Asian American Pan-Ethnic Identity: Pluralized Meanings of a Racial Label." *Sociological Perspectives* 51 (2008): 541–61.

Peery, Destiny, and Galen V. Bodenhausen. "Black + White = Black: Hypodescent in Reflexive Categorization of Racially Ambiguous Faces." *Psychological Science* 19 (2008): 973–77.

Pew Research Center. "Multiracial in America: Proud, Diverse, and Growing in Numbers." Last modified June 11, 2015. www.pewsocialtrends.org.

Pinter, A. T., et al. "It Matters How and When You Ask: Self-Reported Race/Ethnicity of Incoming Law Students." *Cultural Diversity and Ethnic Minority Psychology* 15 (2009): 51–66.

Piper, Adrian. "Passing for White, Passing for Black." *Transition* 58 (1992): 4–32.

Portes, Alejandro, and Dag MacLeod. "What Shall I Call Myself? Hispanic Identity Formation in the Second Generation." *Ethnic and Racial Studies* 19 (1996): 523–47.

Post, Deborah Waire. "The Salience of Race." *Touro Law Review* 15 (1999): 351–87.

"Questions on the Blake Assault." *Qatar Tribune*, September 16, 2015. www.archive.qatar-tribune.com.

Renn, Kristen A. "Creating and Re-Creating Race: The Emergence of Racial Identity as a Critical Element in Psychological, Sociological, and Ecological Perspectives on Human Development." In *New Perspectives on Racial Identity Development: Integrating Emerging Frameworks*. 2nd ed., edited by Charmaine L. Wijeyesinghe and Bailey W. Jackson III, 33–50. New York: NYU Press, 2012.

Rich, Camille Gear. "Elective Race: Recognizing Race Discrimination in the Era of Racial Self-Identification." *Georgetown Law Journal* 102 (2014): 1501–72.

Rives, Scot. "Multiracial Work: Handing Over the Discretionary Judicial Tool of Multiracialism." *UCLA Law Review* 58 (2011): 1303–40.

Román, Miriam Jiménez. "Looking at That Middle Ground: Racial Mixing as Panacea?" In *A Companion to Latina/o Studies*, edited by Juan Flores and Renato Rosaldo, 325–36. Malden, MA: Blackwell, 2007.

Root, Maria P. P. "Bill of Rights for Racially Mixed People." *Drmariapproot.com*, 1993. www.drmariaroot.com.

Root, M. P. P. "Factors Influencing the Variation in Racial and Ethnic Identity of Mixed-Heritage Persons of Asian Ancestry." In *The Sum of Our Parts: Mixed-Heritage Asian Americans*, edited by T. K. Williams-Leon and C. L. Nakasima, 61–70. Philadelphia: Temple University Press, 2001.

Ross, Janel. "The Curious Case of Shaun King, Blogger and Conservative Media Target." *Washington Post*, August 21, 2015. www.washingtonpost.com.

Roth, Wendy. "Racial Mismatch: The Divergence between Form and Function in Data for Monitoring Racial Discrimination of Hispanics." *Social Science Quarterly* 91 (2010): 1288–1309.

Russell, Katheryn K. *The Color of Crime: Racial Hoaxes, White Fear, Black Protectionism, Police Harassment, and Other Macroaggressions.* New York: NYU Press, 1998.

Sanchez, Diana T., and Courtney M. Bonam. "To Disclose or Not to Disclose Biracial Identity: The Effect of Biracial Disclosure on Perceiver Evaluations and Target Responses." *Journal of Social Issues* 65 (2009): 129–49.

Sarich, Vincent, and Frank Miele. *Race: The Reality of Human Differences.* Boulder, CO: Westview, 2004.

Saulny, Susan, and Jacques Steinberg. "On College Forms, a Question of Race, or Races, Can Perplex." *New York Times*, June 13, 2011. Accessed September 14, 2015. www.nytimes.com.

Sekulow, Jay Alan, and Walter M. Weber. "*Fisher v. University of Texas at Austin*: The Incoherence and Unseemliness of State Racial Classification." *University of Miami Business Law Review* 24, n. 11 (2015): 91–98.

Senna, Danzy, "Mulatto Millennium: Since When Did Being the Daughter of a WASP and a Black-Mexican Become Cool?" *Salon.com*, July 24, 1998. Accessed June 12, 2017. www.salon.com.

Sexton, Jared. *Amalgamation Schemes: Antiblackness and the Critique of Multiracialism*. Minneapolis: University of Minnesota Press, 2008.

Simon, Patrick, Victor Piché, and Amélie Gagnon, eds. *Social Statistics and Ethnic Diversity: Cross-National Perspectives on Classifications and Identity Politics*. New York: Springer, 2015.

Smith, James P., and Finis Welch. "Affirmative Action and Labor Markets." *Journal of Economic Issues* 2 (1984): 280–301.

Spencer, Rainier. *Reproducing Race: The Paradox of Generation Mix*. Boulder, CO: Lynne Rienner, 2011.

Spickard, Paul. "Does Multiraciality Lighten? Me-Too Ethnicity and the Whiteness Trap." In *New Faces in a Changing America: Multiracial Identity in the 21st Century*, edited by Loretta I. Winters and Herman L. DeBose, 289–300. Thousand Oaks, CA: Sage, 2003.

Spiegel, Sarah. "Prison Race Rights: An Easy Case for Segregation." *California Law Review* 95 (2007): 2261–93.

Squires, Catherine R. *Dispatches from the Color Line: The Press and Multiracial America*. Albany: State University of New York Press, 2007.

Stanley, Doug. "Census Bureau to Test Revised Race Categories." *Tampa Tribune*, June 4, 1996. Available in 1996 WL 10230771.

Stevens, Mitchell L. *Creating a Class: College Admissions and the Education of Elites*. Cambridge, MA: Harvard University Press, 2007.

Stewart, Dafina-Lazarus. "Know Your Role: Black College Students, Racial Identity, and Performance." *International Journal of Qualitative Studies in Education* 28 (2014): 238–58.

Stone, Kerri Lynn. "Taking in Strays: A Critique of the Stray Comment Doctrine in Employment Discrimination Law." *Missouri Law Review* 77 (2012): 149–97.

Streeter, Caroline A. "The Hazards of Visibility: 'Biracial' Women, Media Images, and Narratives of Identity." In *New Faces in a Changing America: Multiracial Identity in the 21st Century*, edited by Loretta I. Winters and Herman L. DeBose, 301–22. Thousand Oaks, CA: Sage, 2003.

Switzer, Cody. "6 Things Charities Should Know about America's Rapid Demographic Shift." *Chronicle of Philanthropy*, June 8, 2017. Accessed June 8, 2017. www.philanthropy.com.

Texeira, Maria Thierry. "The New Multiracialism: An Affirmation of or an End to Race as We Know It." In *New Faces in a Changing America: Multiracial Identity in the 21st Century*, edited by Loretta I. Winters and Herman L. DeBose, 21–37. Thousand Oaks, CA: Sage, 2003.

Townsend, S. S. M., H. R. Markus, and H. B. Berg Sicker. "My Choice, Your Categories: The Denial of Multiracial Identities." *Journal of Social Issues* 65 (2009): 185–204.

Transfer of Responsibility for Certain Statistical Standards from OMB to Commerce, Dep't of Commerce, Directives for the Conduct of Federal Statistical Activities, Directive No. 15, Race and Ethnic Standards for Federal Statistics and Administrative Reporting. 43 Fed. Reg. 19,260 (1978).

Velasquez-Manoff, Moises. "What Biracial People Know." *New York Times*, March 5, 2017. Sunday Review 1. Accessed June 12, 2017. www.nytimes.com.

Vobejda, Barbara. "Census Expands Options for Multiracial Families." *Washington Post*, October 30, 1997.

Walker, Alamina R. "Choosing to Be Multiracial in America: The Sociopolitical Implications of the "Check All That Apply" Approach to Race Adopted in the 2000 U.S. Census." *Berkeley La Raza La Journal* 21 (2011): 61–91.

Walsh, Eileen T. "The Ideology of the Multiracial Movement: Dismantling the Color Line and Disguising White Supremacy?" In *The Politics of Multiracialism: Challenging Racial Thinking*, edited by Heather M. Dalmage, 219–35. Albany: State of New York Press, 2004.

Webster, Yehudi O. *The Racialization of America.* New York: St. Martin's, 1992.

Williams, Kim M. "Linking the Civil Rights and Multiracial Movements." In *The Politics of Multiracialism: Challenging Racial Thinking*, edited by Heather M. Dalmage, 88. Albany: State University of New York Press, 2004.

Williams, Kim M. *Mark One or More: Civil Rights in Multiracial America.* Ann Arbor: University of Michigan Press, 2006.

Worrell, Frank C. "Nigrescence Attitudes in Adolescence, Emerging Adulthood, and Adulthood." *Journal of Black Psychology* 34 (2008): 156–78.

INDEX

acting white, 96

administrative law judge (ALJ): Bracken claim before HUD, 58; in Jouhari case, 57; White family claim before HUD, 64

adoption, x; of foster children, xi

affirmative action, 4, 43; *Fisher I*, 102–3; *Fisher II* and UT policy of, 103; multiracials undergraduate students benefit from, 107–8; racial inclusion policies challenged in, 102, 103–4; Supreme Court litigation on, 7, 102–9; University of Michigan policy of, 101–2

African Americans: discrimination legal protections, 12; interracial marriage and light skin tone, 30; multiracial claimants distinctive from, 35; multiracial discrimination within race of, 30–35; slavery sexual violence and light skin tone, 30

Afro-Latina, ix

Afro-Puerto Rican, ix–xii

Akron police department, 77–79

Alexander, Angela, 65

Alito, Justice, 103

ALJ. *See* administrative law judge

Allied Educational Foundation, 104

ALPHA HQ, white supremacy movement goals of, 55–57

Amalgamation Schemes (Sexton), 1

amicus curiae briefs (friend of the court), 103–4

Ancestry.com, 1

anti-black bias, 19–21; in *Smith v. CA, Inc.*, 19, 23; in *Watkins v. Hospitality Group Management, Inc.*, 23–25

anti-black conception: of hair, xi–xiii; of Puerto Ricans and Latin Americans, x–xi

antidiscrimination law: Brown, C., lawsuit and, 1–2; on claimants treatment not personal racial identity, 92; comparators in, 12, 26–28; dignity-focused approach to, 114–16; filing time extensions, for multiracial claimants, 92; fluid identity discrimination and, 4–5; introduction to, 9–12; litigation and summary judgment, 92; mixed-race racial identity claimants and, 90; multiracial category lack in, 3; multiracial discrimination and, 8–9; multiracial failings and, 9–15; public goods access and, 113; racial categories and, 12–14, 92; racial mixture complication in, 1–15; as unidirectional, 112; viable multiracial claimants in, 38

anti-mixture bias case: in criminal justice system, 89–90; in employment discrimination, 35–38; in housing discrimination, 55–57

anti-white discrimination, 27

appearances, racial ambiguity in, ix, 2, 48–49, 96, 108

Asian Americans, discrimination legal protections, 12, 14

Asian multiracials, 25–26

Asians, racial or ethnic identification formation of, 97

bad hair (*pelo malo*), xi–xii

Baird, John, 42

ABOUT THE AUTHOR

Tanya Katerí Hernández is the Archibald R. Murray Professor of Law at Fordham University School of Law, where she is an Associate Director of the Center on Race, Law & Justice as its Head of Global and Comparative Law Programs and Initiatives. She received her A.B. from Brown University and her J.D. from Yale Law School.